THE MALBONE STREET WRECK

THE MALBONE

STREET WRECK

BRIAN J. CUDAHY

Fordham University Press
New York
1999

Library of Congress Cataloging-in-Publication Data

Cudahy, Brian J.
    The Malbone Street Wreck / Brian Cudahy.—1st ed.
        p.   cm.
    Includes bibliographical references and index.
    ISBN 0-8232-1931-3 (hardcover).—ISBN 0-8232-1932-1 (pbk.)
    1. Malbone Street Wreck, New York, N.Y., 1918.   2. Subways—
Accidents—New York (State)—New York—History.   3. Brooklyn (New
York, N.Y.)—History.   I. Title.
HE4381.C8   1999
363.12'2—dc21   99-25764
                                                                              CIP

Printed in the United States of America
03   02   01   00   99   5   4   3   2   1
First Edition

CONTENTS

MAPS

ILLUSTRATIONS

TABLES

PREFACE

In the early evening hours of Friday, November 1, 1918, a five-car rapid transit train filled with hundreds of homeward-bound, rush-hour passengers left the tracks at the foot of a short, downhill grade in Brooklyn, New York, and crashed into the side of a new concrete and steel tunnel. Ninety-three people lost their lives in this tragedy that has since been known as the Malbone Street Wreck. This is the story of that terrible evening and the events surrounding it.

Growing up in Brooklyn, I vividly recall continual references in my family to three 20th-century tragedies, each of which taught a different lesson. The first was the Lindbergh kidnapping of 1932. This event resulted in constant admonitions for caution: there were people out there with evil intentions for whom we must always be on the alert. The second event was the tragic sinking of RMS *Titanic* in April 1912. Its lesson was more fatalistic than anything else: sometimes even the most careful plans and the very best efforts are for naught. The year after this disaster my mother crossed the North Atlantic aboard RMS *Baltic* and RMS *Celtic*, White Star Line fleet mates of the *Titanic*. She often spoke of passengers' gathering on deck for a religious service as they steamed past the site of the sinking. The third tragic incident that I recall being discussed in our home was the Malbone Street Wreck of 1918. Its message was less clear. My family responded with anger, even outrage. Innocent people died because other people failed to do their jobs properly. My mother, who was almost 11 years old at the time, lost two cousins on the ill-fated train.

As I grew older, I learned more about the Malbone Street Wreck. Much of what I heard was incomplete, distorted, and even incorrect. As often happens with events that produce broadscale social trauma, early imprecision and unfounded speculation quickly became accepted as truth and took on the aura of dogma.

I always knew exactly *where* the accident happened, and for six years of my life—four years of high school and two of college—travel to and from school required me to pass the site twice each day. Indeed, my homeward-bound ride retraced the last 1.4 miles of the tragic trip of November 1, 1918—including passage around the very curve and into the same tunnel where the ill-fated train came to grief. Whatever other matters may have been holding my immediate attention as my train moved slowly down the hill and wound its way into the Malbone Street tunnel—conversing with schoolmates, analyzing the previous day's box score, making plans for the weekend, or simply daydreaming—some part of me always took note that the train was traveling through a place that was special.

In more recent years, as I have studied the Malbone Street Wreck in some detail, I have identified three themes. None is remarkable, yet each is important. First, the Malbone Street Wreck is a quintessential Brooklyn story. The narrative that follows features Coney Island, Prospect Park, Ebbets Field, Flatbush, Kings Highway, Greenwood Cemetery, Brighton Beach, Park Slope, Atlantic Avenue, the Brooklyn Bridge, the Academy of Music, and Fulton Ferry. Second, the Malbone Street Wreck allows us to examine one very particular moment in the history of urban transportation in the United States with rare precision. Tragedies such as this one often leave behind a quantity of documentary material that otherwise might never have been collected and retained. An examination of urban transportation in Brooklyn circa 1918 reveals change, the real social tension that brought change about, and all the human uncertainty felt by the people who were the agents of that change—mayors, union leaders, judges, federal officials, clergy, company presidents, lawyers, police officers, physicians, and transit riders. Third, the Malbone Street Wreck—terrible and awful as it was—deserves to be better known than it has been.

Unfortunately, the story that follows is not a definitive account of the Malbone Street Wreck. Too much remains unknown, too much lies beyond my grasp, and too many questions are answered imperfectly. Somewhere out there—perhaps in a public archive, but more likely in private hands—documents may exist that will allow further progress toward a definitive account. A series of criminal trials was held following the accident, and the transcripts of these proceedings would be quite valuable. However, if any were ever prepared, I have been unable to locate them—despite diligent efforts that included excursions into dusty basement file rooms of several courthouses.

Even so objective a matter as the precise number of fatal casualties the Malbone Street Wreck produced has been obscured and distorted by factors touched upon in chapter 6. Should this account bring the day closer when unanswered questions associated with the Malbone Street Wreck can be resolved, it will have served a useful purpose.

Because they are so numerous, I will refrain from mentioning all of the many people and institutions who have given me direction and assistance in my efforts to learn more about the Malbone Street Wreck. I will make some exceptions, though. The Archives of the City of New York proved to be a repository of extraordinary value. I must also mention the National Archives and offer three quiet cheers for a federal government that is often criticized and maligned, but at least has the good sense to save the evidence of its activities and make it available to interested parties with a minimum of fuss and bother. Finally, my former classmate and longtime friend Don Harold—a Brooklynite nonpareil—has once again been most generous in sharing his thoughts about New York transit matters with me.

What follows, then, is the story of Brooklyn's Malbone Street Wreck—as best I am able to tell it.

THE MALBONE STREET WRECK

CHAPTER 1
November 1, 1918

It was November 1, 1918, the day of the Malbone Street Wreck, and the Great War was almost over. Armistice would be declared on November 11, and speculation about the long-anticipated event dominated newspapers in Brooklyn and throughout the United States. "Teuton Collapse Hourly Expected" was a typical headline that day.[1]

Although the war's end was clearly in sight, its cost had yet to be fully calculated. Information released in Washington, D.C., each day added more and more names to the list of the nation's war dead. New draft calls continued to be issued, and citizens were still being asked to help the war effort by subscribing to Liberty Bonds. On the day the of the Malbone Street Wreck, the U.S. Military Academy at West Point graduated 511 new second lieutenants in its fourth class of the year. The academy's ordinary curriculum had been drastically shortened to ensure that American Expeditionary Forces fighting in Europe would have adequate numbers of young officers to lead the doughboys into battle. In addition, Americans were encouraged to support their troops in ways that seem unusual today. For example, people were asked to save and contribute ordinary peach pits to the war effort because they contained a substance useful in the manufacture of gas masks.

Although the fields of battle were thousands of miles removed from daily life in the United States, there were frequent reminders on the home front that these were not ordinary times. For instance, on October 27, 1918—five days before the Malbone Street Wreck—the nation set its clocks back an hour to conclude a summer-long effort to "save" an hour of daylight to assist industrial production. This was the first time that this annual autumn ritual ever took place in the United States.

The Great War was not the only cause of extraordinary casualties for Americans—and for Brooklynites—in the fall of 1918. An epidemic of Spanish influenza was taking a terrible toll. When all the counting was done, 320,710 Americans were listed as fatal casualties of the First World War. The influenza epidemic of 1918, on the other hand, claimed more than a half-million U.S. lives within a few short months. One of these deaths—that of a frail, three-year-old girl who died in Brooklyn on October 25, 1918, seven days before the Malbone Street Wreck—is perhaps a very important part of the background of the tragic accident.

By November 1, it was beginning to appear that the epidemic had peaked; reported new cases, as well as deaths attributed to the onslaught, were decreasing daily. But New York residents were still feeling the impact of the epidemic. The New York Telephone Company, whose ranks of operators were seriously depleted by sickness, ran a newspaper advertisement on November 1 that read, "Avoid Telephoning During the Epidemic." A more indelible effect of the epidemic is seen in an advertisement taken out by a local undertaker: "Caskets in Variety Still Available."[2]

Despite wars and plagues and all their attendant horror, Americans still enjoyed their ordinary pastimes in the autumn of 1918. The major league baseball season ended early that year. Wartime travel restrictions had caused the season to be cut short by 25 games or so and, almost two months earlier on September 11, the Boston Red Sox defeated the Chicago Cubs, four games to two, to win the World Series. The accomplishment has assumed legendary proportions among Boston baseball fans in the years since 1918. Despite many close calls, as of this writing the Red Sox have yet to win another World Series.

The hometown Brooklyn Dodgers, playing in newly built Ebbets Field, finished fifth in the National League that year, even though left fielder Zack Wheat, a future member of the Baseball Hall of Fame, led the league with a .335 batting average. On the evening of November 1, 1918, Ebbets Field would be used as an aid station for passengers injured in the Malbone Street Wreck. Home plate was less than 350 yards from the site of the disaster.

Football, of course, was the sport of the season on November 1. In addition to an upcoming weekend of promising intercollegiate action by local teams—Columbia versus Amherst and Fordham versus St. John's—Brooklyn fans were looking forward to an important schoolboy match scheduled for the following Tuesday, Election Day, an academic holiday. Manual Training was to take on Erasmus Hall in the feature game of a high school doubleheader at Ebbets Field. (Erasmus would win, 12 to 0.)

More than high school football would be contested on Election Day. It was not a presidential year; Woodrow Wilson had been elected to his second term two years earlier in 1916. But there was a spirited contest under way for the office of governor of the state of New York, even though on November 1 Republican incumbent Charles S. Whitman was regarded as a solid favorite to win a third two-year term. His Democratic challenger, Alfred E. Smith, was then serving as president of the New York City Board of Aldermen. Smith began his formal campaign on October 20 with an outdoor rally at Lafayette and Duane streets in his home borough of Manhattan. As part of his platform, Smith called for complete municipal ownership of all city mass transit lines rather than the operation of such services by private corporations, as was then the practice. When Smith scored a narrow upset victory over Whitman on November 5, the Malbone Street Wreck was cited as a factor. "Brighton Tragedy Reflex Seen in Flatbush Swing to Democratic Candidates," headlined the *Brooklyn Eagle*.[3]

On the same Friday evening that the Malbone Street Wreck took place, and with the election a mere four days away, Smith and the rest of the Democratic ticket attended a rally at the Brooklyn Academy of Music on Lafayette Avenue. Scheduled to address the partisan crowd that night was an up-and-coming, 26-year-old New York Democrat who was serving as assistant secretary of the navy in President Wilson's administration. However, a sudden flurry of war-related business in Washington forced young Franklin D. Roosevelt to forgo the train ride up to New York that day. It is quite possible that some early-arriving Democrats at the Academy of Music that evening rode aboard the very train that was later involved in the Malbone Street Wreck. An elevated train station at Fulton Street and Lafayette Avenue where the fatal train stopped at 6:26 P.M. was but a block away from the Academy of Music.

Possibly the most interesting feature of the upcoming state election was the fact that it would be the first in New York history in which the electorate was not all male. At the national level, full suffrage was still in the future. The 19th Amendment would not be sent to the states for ratification until June 4, 1919, a process that was certified on August 26 of the following year. On the evening the

Malbone Street Wreck took place in Brooklyn, though, women throughout New York were preparing to vote in their first statewide election.

Entertainment less participatory than either athletics or politics was also on tap on November 1, 1918. Loew's Metropolitan Theater in downtown Brooklyn, for instance, was featuring *The Romance of Tarzan* on the screen, plus a complete stage show. At 6:21 P.M., the ill-fated train en route to disaster at Malbone Street passed within 20 yards of the theater's marquee as it rumbled along the Fulton Street elevated line directly in front of the famous Brooklyn movie hall.

The nation's business and commerce of November 1, 1918, often reflected war-related adjustments. The American Electric Railway Association, a trade organization of the public transit industry, normally held a gala, multiday convention each fall. In 1918, because of the war, a simple one-day business meeting was substituted. It was called to order in the Engineering Societies Building in Manhattan on November 1, and executives from companies throughout Canada and the United States discussed matters of mutual concern, looking ahead to the changes their industry would have to confront once the Great War was concluded. They did not like what they saw. A committee resolution was passed calling on all member companies to see to the swift sale of their properties to the public sector. Just hours before the Malbone Street Wreck occurred, the principal trade association of the North American mass transit industry concluded that the industry had no future as a corporate enterprise in post-war America.[4]

Hours before the Malbone Street Wreck took place in Brooklyn, a key 50-issue index on the New York Stock Exchange closed at 75.60, up 0.16 from the day before. The sun rose in New York on November 1, 1918, at 6:25 A.M. and it set at 4:54 P.M. The day's high tides, as recorded off Governor's Island, were at 6:20 A.M. and 6:39 P.M., the latter a mere three minutes before the accident happened four miles inland. The high temperature for the day was 56 degrees, reached at 1:15 P.M. By six o'clock, less than an hour before the crash, it had fallen to 49 degrees, and at 11:00 P.M., with the work of evacuating dead and injured from the Malbone Street Wreck almost complete, the low temperature for the day was recorded, a brisk 45 degrees. November 1, 1918, was clear and fair, although a bit cooler than normal for that time of year in Brooklyn. Not a trace of precipitation was recorded in the New York metropolitan area on the day the Malbone Street Wreck took the lives of 93 people aboard a five-car rapid transit train.

NOTES

1. *New York Times* (November 1, 1918), 1.

2. *Brooklyn Eagle* (November 1, 1918), 8; *New York Times* (November 1, 1918), 15.

3. *Brooklyn Eagle* (November 6, 1918), 1.

4. The action was widely reported in the mass transit trade press and also drew coverage in the general press. See "Proceedings of the New York Conference," *Electric Railway Journal* 52 (1918): 789–97; *Washington Post* (November 2, 1918), 9; *New York Herald* (November 2, 1918), 9.

CHAPTER 2

The Railway

Today, the Brighton Beach Line is an important rapid transit route of New York City Transit, the public agency responsible for running the city's subway system. Originating in Coney Island and served by the D and Q trains, the Brighton Beach Line connects residential communities throughout the Flatbush area of Brooklyn with commercial and business districts of downtown Brooklyn and Manhattan; it features continuing service to the Bronx and Queens, as well. In 1918, when the Malbone Street Wreck took place along the very same Brighton Beach Line, the operating agency was the privately owned Brooklyn Rapid Transit Company, more commonly known as the BRT.

The Brighton Beach Line has been in daily operation for well over a century. The first train to operate over the route did so on Tuesday afternoon, July 2, 1878—decades before the BRT came on the scene and long before anyone ever heard of New York City Transit. Rutherford B. Hayes was then the nation's chief executive, having won a fiercely contested election against New York's Samuel B. Tilden two years earlier by the narrowest margin in U.S. history, one electoral vote. The Brighton Beach Line of 1878 was anything but the heavy-duty electrified railway of today—or of 1918, for that matter.

The inaugural train was hauled by a steam locomotive named the *John A. Lott*, in honor of a Kings County judge who was the company's first and by this time former president, and it was appropriately decorated with flags and bunting for the ceremonial occasion. It left a station at the southern end of Prospect Park at 5:00 P.M. and reached Brighton Beach less than 14 minutes later. "The big engine . . . puffed and snorted at the station . . . as if impatient to start away on the wings of the wind," reported the *Brooklyn Eagle*. The initial portion of the trip was through tunnels and cuts 50 feet deep from which "nothing but the sky was visible." Then the train emerged into open country dotted with neat farmhouses that featured blooming kitchen gardens surrounded by fertile potato and melon patches.

A two-car train heading for Manhattan Beach on a parallel railroad track was overtaken and passed by the fast-stepping inaugural special. Once the trip was concluded, and after a second ceremonial train from Prospect Park had steamed into Brighton Beach several minutes behind the first one, a festive supper of cold meats was served at the Brighton Beach Hotel to more than 1,000 invited guests. Judge Lott addressed the guests, as did his successor as president of the new railway, James N. Smith.[1]

The corporate mission of the new company was to link built-up sections of Kings County with a fashionable seaside hotel at Brighton Beach. In fact, railway and seaside hotel were a joint venture, the latter owned by the former. "The great resort . . . in the immediate future bids fair to outstrip in popularity its rivals on both sides of the Atlantic," claimed the *Brooklyn Eagle* on the day the enterprise, railway and resort, opened for business.[2] The concession for operating the hotel was subcontracted by the railway company to a pair of experienced New York restaurant and hotel operators. One was a man by the name of Breslin; the other was Abram M. Sweet, a Quaker who opened his first New York restaurant in 1845 and whose name still adorns a famous seafood house in lower Manhattan.

The Brooklyn, Flatbush and Coney Island Railroad, as the company was called, was incorporated nine years earlier on June 25, 1869.[3] It was one of several undertakings in 19th-century Kings County that were known as excursion railways. Although they evolved into commuter-oriented rapid transit services in the 20th century, their original purpose was to link the city of Brooklyn with such breezy beachfront resorts as Coney Island, Sheepshead Bay, Bath Beach, Canarsie, Manhattan Beach, and Brighton Beach. Their trains normally ran throughout the year, but their principal business was seasonal travel to the various beaches. Table 1 identifies the principal 19th-century excursion railways of Kings County.

These 19th-century excursion railways were largely built through lightly settled territory on the outskirts of Brooklyn proper and did not extend their services into the residential and commercial heart of the city. Various reasons are cited to explain this state of affairs, all having degrees of validity: civic opposition to soot-spewing steam locomotives operating in residential areas, pressure from existing street railway companies whose horse-drawn vehicles would be forced to compete with the new railways, the sheer expense of build-

TABLE 1: The 19th-Century Excursion Railways of Kings County

Railroad	Date Opened	Northern Terminal	Southern Terminal
Brooklyn, Bath and Coney Island[a]	1862	25th Street and Fifth Avenue	Coney Island
Brooklyn, Canarsie and Rockaway Beach[b]	1865	Fulton and Atlantic	Canarsie
Prospect Park and Coney Island	1875	20th Street and Ninth Avenue	Coney Island
New York and Manhattan Beach[c]	1876	Long Island City	Manhattan Beach
New York and Sea Beach[d]	1877	Foot of 65th Street	Coney Island
Brooklyn, Flatbush and Coney Island	1878	Flatbush and Atlantic	Brighton Beach

[a] Later called Brooklyn, Bath and West End Railroad; a second northern terminal was established at the foot of 39th Street around 1887.

[b] Major sections now part of New York City Transit's L Line; only excursion railway of those listed that did not serve Coney Island.

[c] Only excursion railway that was abandoned and not converted into a rapid transit line; company also operated trains between Manhattan Beach and the foot of 65th Street in Bay Ridge.

[d] Partial service instituted during summer of 1877; no further service until summer of 1879.

ing a railroad right-of-way through densely settled areas, and the very fact that the railways were not geared to serve year-round markets.

As a result, the excursion railways built their "in-town" terminals on the periphery of Brooklyn's residential core and in most cases beyond the corporate limits of the city of Brooklyn—a municipality that was not as large in 1880 as the Borough of Brooklyn is today. (The Borough of Brooklyn came into existence when the older city of Brooklyn and other political entities were incorporated into a new and expanded New York City—often called Greater New York—on January 1, 1898.) Nineteenth-century passengers had to rely on horsecars operated by various street railway companies to travel from their homes in Brooklyn proper to seashore-bound railroad trains at the city's edge. The New York and Sea Beach Railroad, forerunner of the N trains that operate over today's Sea Beach Line, used an alternate scheme. Its trains to and from Coney Island terminated on the shore of Upper New York Bay in the vicinity of today's 65th Street, where passengers to and from Manhattan had access to side-wheel steamboats—in addition to street railways—for the final (or initial) portion of their journey. The Brooklyn, Bath and West End Railroad eventually provided its patrons with a similar waterborne option at the foot of 39th Street in Brooklyn. Neither railway's trackage, though, reached into the heart of the city of Brooklyn (see map 1).

On July 2, 1878, when the first Brooklyn, Flatbush and Coney Island train inaugurated service over the Brighton Beach Line, it ran from an "in-town" terminal adjacent to the intersection of Flatbush and Ocean avenues at the southeast corner of Prospect Park, the Willink Entrance to the park. The park entrance was named for a family who once owned a fashionable home on Ocean Avenue opposite Prospect Park and adjacent to where the Prospect Park station would be built. The home later became the Hotel Melrose and catered to passengers heading for Brighton Beach aboard the new company's trains. From this point in the town of Flatbush, just beyond Brooklyn's city limits, the Atlantic Ocean and Brighton Beach were a little more than six miles away across sparsely settled flatlands to the south. Passengers bound for Brighton Beach from central Brooklyn could reach the Willink Entrance of Prospect Park from downtown aboard horse-drawn streetcars of the Flatbush Avenue Railway, a company whose carbarn and stable were on the east side of Flatbush Avenue just beyond the station of the new excursion railway.[4] As the inaugural train of the Brooklyn, Flatbush and Coney Island Railroad was boarding passengers in the station at Flatbush and Ocean avenues on the afternoon of July 2, 1878, it was a mere trainlength away from the spot where the Malbone Street Wreck would happen 40 years later.

Investors behind the Brooklyn, Flatbush and Coney Island Railroad believed they had a way of getting their trains closer to the heart of commercial and residential Brooklyn than the other excursion railways. Even as the railroad was inaugurating service on that July day, workers were completing a project that would bring the new company's trains closer to the source of its traffic. Any alignment

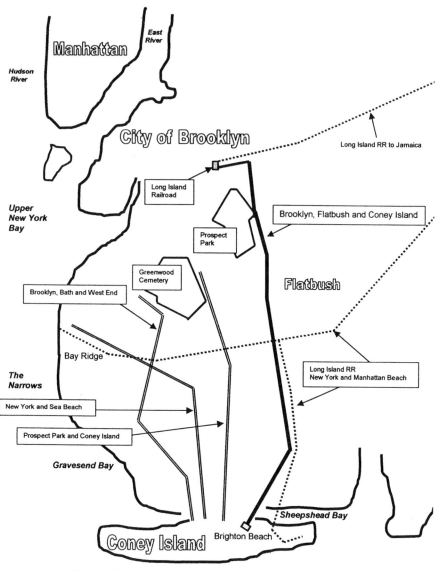

Manhattan

East River

Hudson River

City of Brooklyn

Long Island RR to Jamaica

Long Island Railroad

Upper New York Bay

Brooklyn, Flatbush and Coney Island

Prospect Park

Greenwood Cemetery

Flatbush

Brooklyn, Bath and West End

Bay Ridge

The Narrows

Long Island RR New York and Manhattan Beach

New York and Sea Beach

Prospect Park and Coney Island

Gravesend Bay

Sheepshead Bay

Coney Island

Brighton Beach

Atlantic Ocean

———————————— Brooklyn, Flatbush and Coney Island Railroad

============ Other Kings County excursion railroads

···················· Long Island Railroad, including New York and Manhattan Beach directly through or adjacent to the greensward of Prospect Park was totally out of the question. Prospect Park had been completed in 1874 as a refuge and retreat from precisely the kind of fast-paced industrialism that the new railway represented. So instead, the route bore slightly to the east away from a straight-line route into downtown Brooklyn and made its way up and over Crown Heights. The right-of-way crossed the city limits that separated what was then the town of Flatbush on the south from the city of Brooklyn on the north, a political boundary that ran on an east-west course in the vicinity of today's Montgomery Street. It was down this same grade from Crown Heights that a five-car train, en route to Brighton Beach on the evening of November 1, 1918, raced out of control and crashed at the foot of the hill.

Cresting Crown Heights and tunneling under the magnificent boulevard called Eastern Parkway, which Frederick Law Olmsted and Calvert Vaux had designed as part of their strategic plan for access to Prospect Park, the new railway made a perpendicular approach to Atlantic Avenue, a major east-west artery. Trains of the Long Island Railroad operated on a fenced-in right-of-way in the middle of Atlantic Avenue, en route from Jamaica and points east to their Brooklyn terminal at Flatbush and Atlantic avenues.[5]

Contractual arrangements had been made between the Brooklyn, Flatbush and Coney Island Railroad and the Long Island Railroad to allow the new excursion railway's trains to enter the older railroad's trackage at this point and terminate its trains in the latter's Brooklyn depot. Flatbush Avenue itself was the shorter and more direct route between the Willink Entrance to Prospect Park and the Long Island's depot. However, the roundabout course over Crown Heights and down to Atlantic Avenue was an effective substitute, even though at 2.3 miles it was slightly longer than the 1.7-mile direct route (see map 1).

On August 19, 1878, a month and a half after the railway opened, the final link was complete and the Brooklyn, Flatbush and Coney Island began running its trains from Brighton Beach over Crown Heights, onto Atlantic Avenue, and into the Long Island Railroad depot at Flatbush and Atlantic—by far the most advantageous Brooklyn terminal any of the Kings County excursion railways would ever enjoy. "The opening of the completed road to the corner of Flatbush and Atlantic avenues considerably increased the traffic over that route, and long into the evening the trains of five and six cars were filled," noted the *Brooklyn Eagle*. "Passengers were delighted with the trip over the new road and poured blessings on the heads of the projectors of the enterprise, which brought Coney Island almost to their very doors," the newspaper continued.[6] Long Island Railroad agents sold tickets to Brighton Beach–bound passengers at Flatbush and Atlantic, and the host railroad retained 20 percent of the proceeds as payment for the use of its facilities.

The Brooklyn, Flatbush and Coney Island Railroad, like other early Kings County excursion railways, operated trains that were hauled by steam engines. Shortly after the company opened for business in the summer of 1878, it maintained a fleet of five such locomotives and operated 40 passenger coaches. Most of these cars were typical railroad-style passenger cars of the day. Some, however, were adapted to meet the unusual needs of a railway whose principal clientele consisted of seasonal travelers headed for the beach. These cars lacked any kind of side walls and were fully open to the summer breezes; passengers sat on wooden benches that ran from one side of the car to the other. Like a fictional vehicle that would later be popularized in the Rogers and Hammerstein musical *Oklahoma!* these open cars on the Brooklyn, Flatbush and Coney Island Railroad were equipped with side curtains "that roll right down, in case there's a change in the weather." With the arrival of autumn each year, the open cars were put in storage until warm weather returned in the spring.

Because Brooklyn, Flatbush and Coney Island steam locomotives were commonly turned around after every trip, the company installed turntables at strategic locations. There was one at Brighton Beach, another at Prospect Park, and a third at Bedford Terminal at Franklin and Atlantic avenues—the point where Brooklyn, Flatbush and Coney Island trains connected with the Long Island Railroad. The Brooklyn, Flatbush and Coney Island was able to use the Long Island's engine facilities—including its turntable—at the latter's Flatbush and Atlantic terminal in downtown Brooklyn. The Brooklyn, Flatbush and Coney Island Railroad hauled a small amount of freight and express but, for all of its days, its principal business was moving passengers. Table 2 provides a statistical profile of the Brooklyn, Flatbush and Coney Island Railroad at the end of its first full fiscal year of operation.

TABLE 2: THE BROOKLYN, FLATBUSH AND CONEY ISLAND RAILROAD

Year ending	September 30, 1879
Number of locomotives	7
Number of passenger cars	44
Number of express, freight, and other cars	8
Length of road (miles)	7.5
Annual train miles	118,500 (passenger)
	1,500 (freight)
Annual passengers	873,960
Annual passenger miles	6,554,700
Annual ton miles (freight)	51,296
Income (all sources)	$203,051.30
Expenses	$100,127.78
Debt service	$55,200.29
Capital outlays to build the road	$1,251,099.27
President	Henry C. Murphy
Executives offices located at	185 Montague Street

Source: Data from Henry V. Poor, *Manual of the Railroads of the United States for 1880* (New York: H. V. and H. W. Poor, 1880), 142.

The corporate relationship between the Brooklyn, Flatbush and Coney Island Railroad and the Long Island Railroad that was so important in providing the excursion railway with an in-town terminal at Flatbush and Atlantic avenues proved to be fragile. The Long Island Railroad has a complex history of mergers, takeovers, and subsidiary companies—which is to say it is cut from the same cloth as virtually all major U.S. railroads. In 1876 an independent company called the New York and Manhattan Beach Railroad had begun operating an excursion-style railway to and from Manhattan Beach at the eastern end of Coney Island on a course that was in part parallel and adjacent to what would become the Brooklyn, Flatbush and Coney Island Railroad two years later. Then, in 1883, when the New York and Manhattan Beach became a subsidiary of the Long Island Railroad, the parent company found itself in the awkward position of providing a direct competitor, the Brooklyn, Flatbush and Coney Island, with an advantageous Brooklyn terminal facility; this arrangement had the potential to attract patrons from the Long Island's own New York and Manhattan Beach.

The New York and Manhattan Beach Railroad was not merely a seasonal excursion railway to the oceanfront. It was also part of a basic, all-year railway link between Bay Ridge and points further east on Long Island; the line to Manhattan Beach was actually a branch line of three-plus miles that left the main line at a place in Flatbush called Manhattan Beach Junction. Trains operated to Manhattan Beach, at various times, from Bay Ridge, from Greenpoint, and from Long Island City. Built in 1876 as a narrow-gauge line, the New York and Manhattan Beach was converted to standard gauge soon afterward. It was the only Kings County excursion railway that was not standard gauge from the outset.

The New York and Manhattan Beach Railroad came into being when New York banking tycoon Austin Corbin took a fancy to the oceanfront area at Manhattan Beach on the eastern end of Coney Island (known as Oriental Point). He needed a swift and dependable way for his friends—and, more importantly, his customers—to reach the two upscale resort hotels he eventually constructed there, the Manhattan Beach Hotel (built in 1877) and the Oriental Hotel (built in 1880). Corbin, who enjoyed the management challenges the world of railroading then represented, soon found that the financially ailing Long Island Railroad was ripe for the taking. Stock deals and other financial transactions were quickly arranged, and in 1880 Corbin became the chief executive of a reorganized Long Island Railroad.[7]

Thus, when Corbin's New York and Manhattan Beach was taken over by the Long Island Railroad in 1882, it was the same Austin Corbin, as president of the Long Island, who orchestrated the deal. The Long Island Railroad then went on to forge a partnership with the mighty Pennsylvania Railroad. It was Corbin, more than any other individual, who molded the once shaky Long Island into the most important and dominant suburban railroad in America—a status it still enjoys.

The upshot of the Long Island Railroad's takeover of the New York and Manhattan Beach was that on December 14, 1883, the former evicted the Brooklyn, Flatbush and Coney Island from its Brooklyn depot after five seasons of service between Brighton Beach and Flatbush and Atlantic avenues and canceled the contract that permitted Brooklyn, Flatbush and Coney Island trains to use Long Island's trackage. The excursion railroad found itself cut back to the Bedford Terminal at Atlantic and Franklin avenues, where it formerly connected with the Long Island. This point was too far from the heart of Brooklyn to generate enough passenger traffic to sustain the excursion railway enterprise. Absent the all-important connection with the Long Island Railroad and the patronage generated at Flatbush and Atlantic avenues, the expense of building the Brooklyn, Flatbush and Coney Island up and over Crown Heights was nothing short of a business folly.

The Brooklyn, Flatbush and Coney Island Railroad would eventually prevail over the Long Island Railroad in court on this matter, but the case was not settled until 1889. While the case was in progress, the excursion railway was unable to use Long Island trackage. By the time the litigation had run its course, transportation had evolved in Brooklyn so as to make the former arrangement irrelevant.

Given competition from the New York and Manhattan Beach Railroad and such other excursion railways as the Prospect Park and Coney Island, the Brooklyn, Flatbush and Coney Island had little chance of profitability in its truncated form.[8] The company entered receivership on January 16, 1884, a month after the Long Island's action. Overcapitalization was cited as the technical reason for the move; in simple terms, the railway had no possibility of taking in enough money over its shortened route to pay its bills and service its debts.

Three years later, in 1887, the company was sold to a group of second-mortgage bond holders of the original company under what was described as an "auction under friendly foreclosure proceedings."[9] The reorganized company was renamed the Brooklyn and Brighton Beach Railroad, and fresh capital became available to restore the line's physical plant, the care and maintenance of which had been neglected during the years the former company had been in receivership. The railway-owned Brighton Beach Hotel was also in need of work, since the ocean was slowly encroaching on the land where the building stood. The hotel was jacked up, and 24 railroad tracks were installed under the 550-by-120-foot wooden structure. With 112 freight cars put in position to bear the weight of the four-story building, the hotel was lowered onto the cars and on April 3, 1888, it was hauled 595 feet inland by six of the company's locomotives. There it would remain for the next 35 years. In addition to dragging the company-owned hotel back from the brink of destruction, the reorganized company made other improvements to the Brighton Beach Line: track was realigned and replaced, as necessary; the below-grade cut south of Prospect Park was rebuilt with stone retaining walls; and a new terminal station was constructed at Brighton Beach.

James J. Jourdan of Brooklyn, who had been a member of the board of directors of the Brooklyn, Flatbush and Coney Island, emerged as president of the reorganized railway. Outwardly, the new railroad retained all the character of the older one. As of June 30, 1890, the company owned eight steam locomotives and 42 passenger cars; its right-of-way between Bedford Terminal and Brighton Beach included 12 bridges or trestles and 13 grade crossings.[10] Behind the scenes, however, new faces were charting the railway's future and the plans they were making would soon radically alter the character of the railway.

In 1896, stockholders of the Brooklyn and Brighton Beach Railroad approved a lease of their property to the Kings County Elevated Company. Kings County Elevated was one of Brooklyn's early deployments of steam-powered railway trains running along steel viaducts built over city streets. In the late-19th century, this form of urban transportation had become necessary in Brooklyn and elsewhere when traffic density and congestion began to turn city travel into a hopeless nightmare. By uniting the line to and from Brighton Beach with the Kings County Elevated, the company was turning the excursion railway into a basic, everyday mass transit service that would serve the growing residential neighborhoods between Prospect Park and Brighton Beach. Its days as a seasonally oriented service whose mission was to speed across this lightly settled territory to the seashore were ending. The potato gardens and melon patches of the 1870s were rapidly becoming unbroken tracts of new homes.[11]

In 1880, two years after the Brooklyn, Flatbush and Coney Island Railroad inaugurated service to and from Brighton Beach, the population of Kings County stood at 599,495. In 1890 it had risen to 838,547; by 1900 it was 1,160,582, almost double the count of 1880. Much of this growth was in areas such as Flatbush, where land was readily available for the construction of new homes.

The city of Brooklyn was also expanding its political boundaries and absorbing previously independent jurisdictions. In 1894, the town of Flatbush became part of the city of Brooklyn, and a referendum was passed that led to the amalgamation of Brooklyn and other cities and towns into a unified New York City on January 1, 1898.

The elevated railways of Brooklyn were operated by two principal companies. Kings County Elevated headed eastward from downtown Brooklyn over Fulton Street; it was organized in 1879, ran its first train in 1888, and was in full operation by 1893. Brooklyn's other elevated railway company, which operated its first train in 1885, involved two once-separate companies—Brooklyn Elevated Railway and Union Elevated Railway—that were eventually combined as the Brooklyn Union Elevated. Among its routes, the company had a major trunk line that operated out of downtown Brooklyn along Myrtle Avenue, parallel to and in competition with Kings County Elevated's Fulton Street Line.

Once the lease of the Brooklyn and Brighton Beach to the Kings County Elevated was executed, the one-time excursion road was extended north from Bedford Terminal at Atlantic Avenue, across the Long Island Railroad at grade, and up a ramp to connect with the Fulton Street elevated line two blocks away. A track connection was soon completed, and the project represented a capital outlay of between $200,000 and $300,000.

On Saturday, August 15, 1896, the Brooklyn and Brighton Beach Railroad and the Kings County Elevated inaugurated through passenger service between Sands Street at the Brooklyn end of the Brooklyn Bridge (which had opened in 1883) and the oceanfront at Brighton Beach. At the Sands Street station, passengers could transfer from steam-powered Brooklyn elevated trains and complete their journey to Manhattan aboard heavy-duty cable trains that crossed the world-famous span.

Trains between Brooklyn Bridge and Brighton Beach ran every 20 minutes from morning through evening, scheduled running time was 35 minutes, and the fare from one end of the line to the other was 10 cents. When passengers detrained at the seashore to stroll the grounds of the Brighton Beach Hotel on that first day of through service, they were serenaded by the musical strains of Seidl's Famous Orchestra.

The Kings County Elevated had an alternative downtown terminal to the Sands Street station at the end of the Brooklyn Bridge; it was located on the bank of the East River at the foot of Fulton Street. Here passengers could transfer to side-wheel ferryboats of the Union Ferry Company for a fast trip across the East River to Manhattan on the Fulton Ferry, as well as to vessels of the Pennsylvania Annex line for a ferry ride that bypassed the congestion of lower Manhattan and went directly to the Jersey City Depot of the Pennsylvania Railroad.[12] (The Pennsylvania Annex ferry was discontinued in 1910 with the opening of Penn Station in Manhattan. A former employee of the company, Charles Thorn, was among the 93 people killed in the Malbone Street Wreck.)

With the amalgamation of Fulton Street and Brighton Beach services, locomotives and rolling stock that the Brooklyn and Brighton Beach Railroad had inherited from the Brooklyn, Flatbush and Coney Island were phased out in favor of slightly smaller equipment built to the specifications of Kings County Elevated. When the Brighton Beach Line was strictly an excursion railway, it used conventional railroad locomotives to haul its trains, full-size engines that were equipped with tenders for carrying water and fuel. In order to operate over elevated lines, lightweight locomotives were needed that could navigate easily around the many sharp curves of the overhead railways. The new locomotives were smaller and not equipped with tenders; they carried fuel and water in on-board tanks and bunkers. These almost diminutive steam locomotives could operate equally well in either direction, and thus could be reversed at the end of the line for a return trip with a minimum of effort. They were known as Forney-type engines—after their designer, Matthias Nace Forney. The Brooklyn elevated lines owned 140 of the little locomotives at the peak of steam-powered elevated operations in the late 1890s.[13] In addition, passenger cars were standardized around a 50-foot design that could operate comfortably over the elevated lines. Cars used by the Brooklyn and Brighton Beach were slightly larger and heavier than operating constraints of the elevated lines allowed, and it seems that none of them joined the Kings County fleet.[14]

The largely untold story of the elevated railways of Kings County is lengthy, not to say convoluted and complex.[15] As matters relate to the Malbone Street Wreck, an important milestone in the history of Brooklyn elevated railways was reached in 1896, the same year that the Brooklyn and Brighton Beach Railroad was united with the Kings County Elevated. On January 18 of that year, papers were filed in Albany for the incorporation of a new entity called the Brooklyn Rapid Transit Company, a firm whose mission was to combine the many independent street, elevated, and excursion railway operations in and around Brooklyn into a unified system. Of six individuals from Brooklyn identified as company directors, one of them—Timothy S.

Williams, a former newspaperman from Ithaca, New York—would later be indicted on four counts of manslaughter for the role he allegedly played in the Malbone Street Wreck.[16]

The major force behind the new BRT was a financial syndicate headed by former New York State Governor Roswell P. Flower. Williams served as Flower's secretary while the latter was the state's chief executive and then joined his former boss in the transportation investment business when Flower's term as governor ended in 1895. Their first venture was a takeover of the Long Island Traction Company in 1895. This was followed by the establishment of the BRT in 1896, as a successor to Long Island Traction.

Although Brooklyn transit passengers would soon come to know and identify the BRT as the agency that ran their trolley cars and their elevated trains, in the world of investments and corporate securities the BRT was a holding company that controlled a number of underlying subsidiaries that actually owned the rolling stock, operated the trains, and were linked together through all manner of long-term leases and other financial arrangements.[17] The Brooklyn and Brighton Beach Railroad was absorbed by the Kings County Elevated, by lease, in 1896. Three years later, the BRT used the corporate structure of the Brooklyn Heights Railroad, a company that had originally been part of Long Island Traction, to take over Kings County Elevated as well as the Brooklyn Union Elevated. In 1912, the BRT established a new company called the New York Consolidated Railroad to serve as the operating entity of its rapid transit trains. Ordinary Brooklyn transit passengers paid little or no mind to this corporate complexity.

After the jointly operated Fulton Street and Brighton Beach lines were brought under formal BRT control in 1899, the new company did away with the steam locomotives that had been hauling trains between the Brooklyn Bridge and Brighton Beach and converted the line to electric power—the new source of energy that was then transforming transportation throughout urban America.[18] Electrification along the Brighton Beach Line was with overhead trolley wire, similar to that used by street railways. The Fulton Street elevated train used a track-level third rail for distributing electric current. Along the route of the old Brooklyn, Flatbush and Coney Island, however, there were many grade crossings and the trackage was dangerously accessible to unwary pedestrians—and even wandering livestock, to the extent that the railroad's service area still had a certain rural and agricultural character to it. Thus, it made more sense to keep the system for distributing electric current out of harm's way by hanging it high over the tracks, rather than placing it next to the running rails. Many of the older Kings County Elevated passenger cars that had been designed and built to be hauled by Forney-type locomotives were equipped with electric motors as part of the steam-to-electricity conversion. Two of these rebuilt cars, in fact, were in the five-car train that crashed in the Malbone Street tunnel on November 1, 1918.

Use of overhead trolley wire along the newly electrified Brighton Beach Line also allowed streetcar companies that had been brought into the BRT family to use the route, in summertime, on their way to Coney Island. "All cars run to Coney Island" was an expression that was often heard in Brooklyn neighborhoods; while it was never literally true, the summer season did see through streetcar service to the oceanfront provided by lines that normally did not go near Coney Island. Some of this seasonal service operated over the Brighton Beach Line; a ramp was built at the Prospect Park station to permit streetcars to descend from street level to the rapid transit tracks below. It remained in use for almost a decade.[19]

At some point—the exact date is uncertain—a four-track repair and storage facility for Brighton Beach Line trains was built on the west side of the right-of-way adjacent to the Sheepshead Bay station. In 1899, the same year that the Brighton Beach Line was electrified, the BRT made arrangements to operate its elevated trains across the Brooklyn Bridge to Manhattan and a terminal on Park Row adjacent to City Hall. BRT elevated trains first supplemented and eventually replaced the original cable railway trains that had been running across the Brooklyn Bridge since it opened in 1883.

Now passengers from the Flatbush area could reach Manhattan without having to change vehicles en route. The one-time excursion railway to Brighton Beach was even further transformed into a year-round, urban rapid transit service.

There were other changes, too; at the southern end of the route, Brighton Beach no longer served as the line's sole terminal. The Prospect Park and Coney Island Railroad—built by Andrew Culver in 1876 and sold to Austin Corbin's Long Island Railroad in 1893—was brought under BRT control in 1899. In 1903 the BRT extended the

Brighton Beach Line westward from Brighton Beach, parallel to the oceanfront and at grade, so it could join the former Prospect Park and Coney Island in the latter's Culver Depot in Coney Island. This extension of slightly less than a mile gave passengers access to the developing amusement areas in the West Brighton section of Coney Island, as well as to Brighton Beach.[20] Culver Depot then became the nerve center for Culver Line and Brighton Beach Line operations under the auspices of a unified BRT.

The BRT realized the need for further improvements on its Brighton Beach Line because the residential territory it served continued to grow. On December 30, 1905, construction began on a project that would substantially upgrade major portions of the line. In 1903, the state legislature had created a Brooklyn Grade Crossing Commission; five members were appointed by the mayor of New York, one by the Long Island Railroad, and one by the BRT-owned Brooklyn Heights Railroad. This body planned a comprehensive program to eliminate grade crossings in Brooklyn, focusing on the BRT's Brighton Beach Line and the Bay Ridge Branch of the Long Island Railroad. The city of New York was to provide half of the money required for the project and the railroads the other half, although the city's contribution could not exceed a million dollars.

This project made the Brighton Beach Line the first of the one-time Kings County excursion railways to benefit from a largely grade-separated right-of-way. The below-grade right-of-way that the old Brooklyn, Flatbush and Coney Island Railroad had originally constructed in the area immediately adjacent to Prospect Park was extended southward to Foster Avenue. At this point, the Brighton Beach Line ascended a short grade and emerged onto a newly built earthen embankment that ran from Avenue H to Sheepshead Bay. South of Sheepshead Bay, the line dropped back to surface operation for the final leg into the terminal at Brighton Beach and beyond to Culver Depot.

Street crossings were eliminated on the below-grade section of the route by having intersecting streets cross the railroad on bridges; they were eliminated along the embankment portion by having cross-streets duck under the right-of-way. Separating the railroad grade permitted the BRT to replace the line's trolley wire north of Sheepshead Bay with a ground-level third rail for the distribution of electric current; this meant that streetcars could no longer use the Brighton

Beach Line en route to Coney Island. Perhaps the most telling change on the line was expansion of the reconstructed section into a four-track railroad featuring both express and local service. The two outside tracks were for the locals, and they made all station stops. The inside tracks were for express trains, and they stopped only at stations featuring special island platforms positioned between the local and express tracks. Such express stops were established at Sheepshead Bay, Kings Highway, and Newkirk Avenue; all other stops—and there were seven of them on the rebuilt section— were for local trains only.

The project was an engineering challenge. The open-cut portions were constructed through relatively built-up residential areas and there was little room adjacent to the right-of-way for construction equipment, staging, and material storage. Regular Brighton Beach Line service had to be maintained during construction. Furthermore, because so many new homes had been built adjacent to the Brighton right-of-way in the Flatbush area, the Grade Crossing Commission determined that it would be less expensive to build the below-grade portion of the line inside a trench lined with perpendicular concrete walls. The traditional method for building a below-grade railway called for gently sloped, earthen sides, supplemented by small retaining walls near the bottom; using such a technique on the Brighton Beach Line would have required substantially more land. Thus, the expense of building concrete walls actually reduced the overall cost of the project since it permitted residential and commercial construction to remain in place up to the edge of the right-of-way.

It was a little easier building the earthen embankment section. There was more elbow room here for crews to work because the embankment traversed less densely settled territory. In addition, Brighton Beach trains were rerouted onto adjacent tracks of the Long Island Railroad's New York and Manhattan Beach during the construction project, although exactly how this rerouting was effected remains unclear. Possibly temporary trolley wire was strung over the Long Island Railroad while construction was under way; perhaps BRT elevated trains were hauled along the Long Island by steam engines.

In any event, the earthen embankment required almost a million cubic yards of new fill for its completion. Of this material, 230,000 cubic yards came from excavating the below-grade open cut on the Brighton Beach Line itself north of Foster Avenue; the remainder was from places where a below-grade right-of-way was built for the Bay Ridge branch of the Long Island Railroad as part of the same effort to eliminate grade crossings. And, if the New York and Manhattan Beach cooperated during the project's construction by allowing Brighton Beach Line trains to use its trackage, the completed new right-of-way atop the new embankment included room for not only the Brighton Beach Line's four-track right-of-way, but also for two tracks of Long Island's subsidiary.[21]

In addition to this major improvement of the Brighton Beach Line south of Prospect Park, sections of the line over Crown Heights between Prospect Park and the connection with the BRT elevated train at Fulton Street were also improved. Grade crossings were eliminated by putting the northern half of the route onto a new elevated structure; the rest of the line remained in its original open cut below the level of surrounding streets. Although this was still a two-track line, sufficient property was acquired along the rebuilt sections to permit expansion to four-track capacity at some future time.[22]

Despite this foresight in 1907, the final upgrading of the Brighton Beach Line to its contemporary configuration would not entail improvements to the original line over Crown Heights between Prospect Park and Fulton Street. Instead, in 1913 agreements were reached that transformed public transportation in New York City completely and forever. The Dual Subway Contracts, as the agreements were called, were a milestone in American urban transportation. An examination of the contracts also provides context for how and why the Malbone Street Wreck happened.

First some background. In 1904, New York City began service on its first underground subway line, a route from City Hall in downtown Manhattan north to Harlem and the Bronx. Built with public funds but operated under long-term lease by the privately owned Interborough Rapid Transit Company, the new subway quickly demonstrated that fast-running, underground mass transit was exactly what the rapidly expanding city needed.[23] Thus, in a negotiation that was completed in March 1913, arrangements were made to expand the city's original subway into a vast, citywide system. Actually, to be more precise, the 1913 agreement called for the construction of two separate rapid transit systems (the dual subway systems)—an expan-

sion of the original Interborough line that opened in 1904 and a
subway system built around a nucleus of the BRT elevated network;
in addition, the "citywide" Dual Subway Contracts called for no
mileage at all in the city's island borough, Staten Island.

The Public Service Commission for the First District of the State
of New York would oversee construction of the $352 million project.
Both the BRT and the Interborough would operate their respective
portions of the new network as profit-seeking enterprises.[24]

The master plan laid out in the Dual Subway Contracts called for
major upgrading and change to the Brighton Beach Line. The contracts would expand the entire line between Prospect Park and
Coney Island into a four-track alignment, just as the BRT itself had
done to portions of the route in 1907. The plan also called for supple-
menting the Brighton Beach Line's original approach to downtown
Brooklyn over Crown Heights and the connection with the Fulton
Street elevated train with a new, two-track subway tunnel that would
begin at Prospect Park and proceed north under Flatbush Avenue.
This is the same route that the Brooklyn, Flatbush and Coney Island
Railroad's surface-running steam engines were unable to use in 1878;
it became feasible in 1913 because electric-powered subway trains
could operate through newly built underground tunnels. This new
route would give Brighton Beach Line trains access to the BRT's
developing subway network at an underground junction near DeKalb
Avenue and Flatbush Avenue Extension in downtown Brooklyn. Service would continue from there—using new bridge and tunnel
links—across the East River into Manhattan, eventually to Queens,
and decades later to the Bronx. It would also permit the line's older,
smaller, and largely wooden elevated-style rapid transit cars to be
replaced by new, heavyweight steel subway equipment.[25]

Before the "Brighton L," as it was often called, could be converted
into an element of the new BRT subway system, major construction
was necessary, including construction of a tunnel under Flatbush
Avenue north from Prospect Park. So as not to disrupt the park itself,
the tunnel was bored from within, thus minimizing the amount of
surface excavation needed along the park's eastern perimeter. A massive, 60-ton roof shield that was 12 feet high and 36 feet wide was
fabricated in West Elizabeth, New Jersey, and erected at the bottom
of a shaft at the tunnel's southern limit near the Willink Entrance

to Prospect Park. As the roof shield was pushed forward by 14 110-ton hydraulic jacks, the tunnel was built in its wake.

This portion of the project, which was under the management of the Degnon Contracting Company, was part of a larger effort to construct the BRT's two-track Brighton Beach Line between Prospect Park and DeKalb Avenue and a four-track extension of the Interborough Rapid Transit Company's Brooklyn Line. The original Manhattan subway of 1904 had been extended to a Brooklyn terminal at Flatbush and Atlantic avenues in 1908; the Dual Subway Contracts would extend it further into residential areas of Brooklyn. Between Flatbush and Atlantic—the site of the Long Island Railroad's Brooklyn terminal—and Grand Army Plaza at the northern end of Prospect Park, a new six-track subway right-of-way was constructed under Flatbush Avenue; it consisted of four outside tracks for the Interborough and two inside tracks for the BRT. This element of the Dual Subway System—technically designated "Section 2A of Route 12"—was built by the Inter-Continental Construction Corporation.[26] At Grand Army Plaza, the Interborough line turned eastward under Eastern Parkway; the BRT's Brighton Beach Line continued southward through the tunnel under Prospect Park that the Degnon Company was building.

Officials initially believed that all this construction would be completed by early 1918, but strikes and other factors forced postponements. Thus, on November 1, 1918—the day of the Malbone Street Wreck—the Brighton Beach Line was still using its older link with the Fulton Street elevated line over Crown Heights while construction work continued on the new subway connection under Flatbush Avenue between Prospect Park and DeKalb Avenue. Prospect Park station was in the process of being transformed from a way station on the line between Fulton Street and Coney Island into a junction where the new line would join the old one.

As was the case during the 1907 upgrade project, regular rapid transit service over the Brighton Beach Line via Crown Heights and the Fulton Street elevated line was maintained during construction. Coordination of the various aspects of the project was critical, so work was done in carefully planned stages; elements of new construction were phased into service as they were ready. One such phase-in took place on September 25, 1918, 36 days before the Malbone Street Wreck. Southbound trains en route to Brighton Beach descending the grade from Crown Heights were routed out of the old tunnel under Malbone Street and Flatbush Avenue that had been in service since 1878; these trains were rerouted into a newly constructed tunnel that would allow them to pass over the subway line under Flatbush Avenue that was still under construction and would eventually become the Brighton Beach Line's new link to downtown Brooklyn. Southbound trains running downhill entered this tunnel at the foot of the hill as they negotiated a 240-foot radius curve to the right, a curve that quickly reversed itself to the left inside the tunnel before emerging as the southbound local track in the Prospect Park station. Together the two elements of this S-curve totaled about 45 degrees.

This routing of southbound trains into the new tunnel allowed construction to begin on the next phase of the project, a new northbound platform at the Prospect Park station. Trains bound for Brighton Beach began using a newly built southbound platform at the Prospect Park station on September 25, at the same time that they began using the new tunnel. Trains bound for Fulton Street continued to use the original tunnel and would do so even after the project was finished. What would eventually become the main passenger entrance to the Prospect Park station at its northern end was still incomplete and would not open until May 1919. On November 1, 1918, the only functioning passenger entrance to the Prospect Park station was at Lincoln Road, to the south.[27]

In terms of the corporate development of the railway, as well as its physical configuration adjacent to the Prospect Park station, the stage is now set for the Malbone Street Wreck.

NOTES

1. Information and quotations from *Brooklyn Eagle* (July 2, 1878), 2. See also *New York Times* (July 2, 1878), 5.

2. Ibid.

3. Capital stock certificates issued by the company show an "incorporation" date of June 25, 1869. Another source claims the company was "organized" on September 13, 1877; see Henry V. Poor, *Manual of the Railroads of the United States* (New York: H. V. and H. W. Poor, 1880), 142 (hereafter referred to as *Poor's Manual*). The Brooklyn, Flatbush and Coney Island Railroad may have been formed by the merger of two proposed excursion

railways—the Flatbush and Coney Island Park and Concourse Railroad Company and the Coney Island and East River Company—before construction began on either; see *New York Times* (June 15, 1879), 1.

4. The first horse-drawn streetcar to carry revenue passengers in Brooklyn did so in 1853. The Flatbush Avenue Railway was founded some years later; it eventually provided service between downtown Brooklyn, Flatbush, and Bergen Beach, operating primarily along what is undoubtedly Brooklyn's most famous thoroughfare, Flatbush Avenue. Later electrified, the Flatbush Avenue Line became part of the Brooklyn City Railroad, and eventually the Brooklyn Rapid Transit Company. Today, New York City Transit's B-41 bus, the Flatbush Avenue route, continues the service pioneered by horse-drawn streetcars of the Flatbush Avenue Railway.

5. A predecessor company of the Long Island Railroad inaugurated service from Atlantic Avenue and the East River to Jamaica in 1836. In 1859, the city of Brooklyn banned steam locomotives from Atlantic Avenue; railroad trains were cut back to East New York, with horsecars providing continuing service into downtown Brooklyn. In 1877, steam-powered Long Island Railroad trains returned to the route, but they terminated at Flatbush and Atlantic avenues, not Atlantic Avenue and the East River. For further information on this interesting railroad, see Vincent F. Seyfried, *The Long Island Railroad: A Comprehensive History* (Garden City, N.Y.: Author, 1961–1975); Mildred H. Smith, *Early History of the Long Island Railroad* (Uniondale, N.Y.: Salisbury, 1958); Ron Ziel and George Foster, *Steel Rails to the Sunrise* (New York: Duell, Sloan and Pearce, 1965).

6. *Brooklyn Eagle* (August 20, 1878), 2. If transit officials today learned that passengers intended to pour anything on their heads, it is unlikely they would expect it to be blessings.

7. For a short, but interesting, account of Corbin, Manhattan Beach, and the New York and Manhattan Beach Railroad, see Edward W. Denny, *The Story of Manhattan Beach* (New York: Hart and Company, 1879).

8. The Prospect Park and Coney Island Railroad ran from the Brooklyn city line at Ninth Avenue and 21st Street, adjacent to Greenwood Cemetery, where connecting service to and from downtown Brooklyn was available aboard horse-drawn streetcars of the Atlantic Avenue Railroad. The railroad line proceeded due south to the West Brighton section of Coney Island, and excursion railway service was inaugurated in 1875. The guiding force behind the venture was Andrew Culver; the line's Coney Island terminal facing Surf Avenue just to the west of its intersection with West Fifth Street came to be called Culver Depot. The Prospect Park and Coney Island Railroad ran parallel to the Brooklyn, Flatbush and Coney Island less than a mile to the west. See "Prospect Park and Coney Island Railroad Company," *Poor's Manual* (1891), 450–1.

9. *Brooklyn Eagle* (August 26, 1887), 2. For additional information on this transaction, see *Documents of the Senate of the State of New York* (Albany, N.Y.: Troy Press,1889), 1:121–6.

10. See "Brooklyn and Brighton Beach Railroad Company," *Poor's Manual* (1891), 75–6.

11. James Jourdan, who became president of the Brooklyn and Brighton Beach Railroad when the company was reorganized in 1887, was also the president of the Kings County Elevated Company.

12. For further information on ferry service in New York, see my book, *Over and Back: The History of Ferryboat Transportation in New York* (New York: Fordham University Press, 1990).

13. For information on Forney-type steam engines, see John H. White Jr., "Spunky Little Devils: Locomotives of the New York Elevated," *Railroad History* 162 (Spring 1990): 20–58.

14. Published rosters of Brooklyn elevated equipment show no cars operating on the elevated lines that were originally owned by the Brooklyn, Flatbush and Coney Island or the Brooklyn and Brighton Beach. See George Rahilly, "The Wooden Cars of the Brooklyn Elevated Railroads," *Headlights* 56 (July-August 1994): 2–13.

15. Rahilly, "Wooden Cars." See also James C. Greller and Edward B. Watson, *The Brooklyn Elevated* (Hicksville, N.Y.: N.J. International, 1987); Karl Groh, "Above the Streets of Brooklyn," *Headlights* 37 (September-November 1975): 2–20; Alan Paul Kahn and Jack May, *The Tracks of New York; No. 2, Brooklyn Elevated Railroads* (New York: Electric Railroaders' Association, 1975); "When the Elevated Was Opened in 1885," *BRT Monthly* (April 1923): 4; "Extensive Improvements in Elevated Car Equipments *(sic)*—Brooklyn Rapid Transit Company," *Street Railway Journal* 24 (August 13, 1904): 222–8; "The Reconstruction Improvements in Equipment of the Brooklyn Elevated Cars," *Street Railway Journal* 24 (August 20, 1904): 252–9; "New Semi-Convertible Cars with Steel Underframes for the Brooklyn Rapid Transit Company," *Street Railway Journal* 25 (May 6, 1905): 804–11.

16. The BRT had six Brooklyn directors: William C. Bryant, Horace C. Duval, William W. Goodrich, John D. Keiley, Clinton L. Rossiter, and Timothy S. Williams. There were also seven directors from New York City: E. L. Button, William F. Creed, Frederick S. Flower, Otto Zonker Jr., Thomas Renwick, Floyd Vail, and James N. Wallace. *New York Times* (January 19, 1896), 7.

17. According to *Poor's Manual* (1900), 944, "As the (BRT) company is simply a business corporation, without authority to operate railroads, the direct management of the system is vested in the Brooklyn Heights R.R. Co."

18. For information on the emergence of electric propulsion on urban railways, see William D. Middleton, *The Time of the Trolley* (Milwaukee: Kalmbach, 1967), 52–73. See also my book, *Cash, Tokens and Transfers* (New York: Fordham University Press, 1990), 35–50.

19. Among the BRT streetcar lines that used the electrified trackage of the Brighton Beach Line for summertime access to Coney Island were the Franklin Avenue Line, the Lorimer Street Line, and the Tompkins Avenue Line.

20. By 1918 Coney Island had lost the status of barrier island it once enjoyed and had evolved into a hammerhead peninsula attached to the Kings County mainland. Thus it remains today. Brighton Beach is part of what might be called the Coney Island land mass—that is, the original island. Today, though, the name Coney Island refers only to the western end of the peninsula. Brighton Beach and Manhattan Beach are sections or neighborhoods on the eastern end. During the 19th century and into the early years of the 20th, that part of Coney Island that is now called Coney Island was generally known as West Brighton.

21. See "The Brighton Beach Improvement of the Brooklyn Heights Railroad," *Street Railway Journal* 29 (May 11, 1907): 830–3.

22. See "The Franklin Avenue Improvement on the Brighton Beach Line of the Brooklyn Rapid Transit Company," *Street Railway Journal* 29 (June 22, 1907): 1104–7.

23. I have written elsewhere of the New York subways and the Dual Subway Contracts; see *Under the Sidewalks of New York*, 2d rev. ed. (New York: Fordham University Press, 1995), 53–70.

24. For further information on the Dual Subway Contracts, see *New Subways for New York: The Dual System of Rapid Transit* (New York: Public Service Commission for the First District, 1913); Clifton Hood, *722 Miles: The Building of the Subways and How They Transformed New York* (New York: Simon and Schuster, 1993), 135–61

25. The standard Brooklyn wooden elevated car was 49 feet long and 8 feet 7 inches wide; see "New Semi-Convertible Cars with Steel Underframes." New steel subway cars developed by the BRT for subway operations were 67 feet long and 10 feet wide. See *Under the Sidewalks of New York*, 67–70.

26. See "Reconstruction of Brighton Beach Line," *BRT Monthly* (August 1917): 9–10; "Reconstruction of the Brighton Beach Line," *Public Service Record* (December 1918), 12–5. For information on construction delays associated with the Brighton Beach Line, see Public Service Commission for the First District, *Report for the Year Ending December 31, 1918* (Albany: J. B. Lyon Company, 1919), 1:148–50.

27. The Brighton Beach Line is built along a north-south axis, and Brigh-

ton Beach–bound trains are clearly headed southward in the Prospect Park–Malbone Street area. In 1918, however, the BRT identified all trains headed away from downtown Brooklyn as *eastbound*, whatever their true compass direction. A Brighton Beach–bound train was thus eastbound, not southbound, in the company's schedules. For clarity's sake in this discussion, Brighton Beach–bound trains are called *southbound*; trains heading toward Fulton Street and downtown Brooklyn are called *northbound*.

CHAPTER 3
The Strike

If there is a single aspect of the Malbone Street Wreck that places the tragedy in a context that is alien to contemporary ways of thinking, it is the state of labor-management relations on the Brooklyn Rapid Transit Company (the BRT) in 1918. Because labor-management relations play such a central role in the events leading up to the accident, it is necessary to note certain events that occurred during the spring and summer of 1918.

The Cleveland-based Brotherhood of Locomotive Engineers, founded in 1863, had a long history with the BRT, going back to the late 19th century when the elevated trains of predecessor companies were hauled by steam locomotives. The relationship was far from happy because the BRT steadfastly refused to recognize any independent labor union as a bona fide bargaining agent for its workers.

Although the company often publicly professed disinterest in whether individual employees joined such a union, as a practical and day-to-day matter the BRT was considerably less open-minded. Management officials often followed suspected employees after work; disciplinary action, usually on trumped-up charges, regularly followed any discovery that a worker was active in union affairs—or, for that matter, had even dropped by a union hall after supper some evening out of pure curiosity.

There was one employee organization, however, that company management permitted BRT workers to join. In fact, membership was mandatory. The organization, which was recognized as a formal representative of the workers, was called the Employes' Benefit Association (the EBA).[1] While it was, indeed, an organization whose mission and function involved the betterment of working conditions and terms of employment for BRT workers, it lacked the independence from management that labor unions such as the Brotherhood of Locomotive Engineers believed was so necessary.

Some officers in the association were elected by the rank and file, but the key post of president of the EBA was appointed by the president of the BRT, Timothy S. Williams. Thus, the organization was anything but an independent voice of and for BRT workers. It was a "company union," to use a term of some opprobrium that was often heard during the early years of the labor movement.

The EBA's agenda included a number of wholesome-enough activities. It sponsored a baseball league for athletically inclined motormen and conductors, although formal league play was suspended during 1917 and 1918 because of the war; it ran an annual boxing tournament; it held railway and steamboat outings for employees and their families; it even had its own 60-piece marching band, a musical aggregation presided over by John Thomas Clisset, a white-bearded drum major who learned martial music as a drummer boy in his native England with the Coldstream Guards and the Lancaster Rifles. While he spent his working hours as an ordinary-enough supervisor on the BRT's streetcar system, after hours and all dressed up in his fancy uniform, Clisset had all the aplomb of John Philip Sousa.

To assist the nation's war effort, in 1918 the EBA undertook a subscription drive among its members to purchase an ambulance for American expeditionary forces fighting in France. So successful was the campaign that the EBA found itself with sufficient resources to buy not one, but two ambulances. Over and above these leisure-oriented and sometimes patriotic activities, the EBA provided a forum for employees to air grievances against their supervisors. Even more important, it was the EBA rather than the BRT that managed and funded what would today be called the fringe-benefit package in which company workers participated—it provided pay for sick days, disability payments, and death benefits. The association raised money for these programs from monthly membership charges; from proceeds raised by outings and excursions; and from profits generated by cafeterias and pool rooms located in BRT depots, the operation of which was also an association responsibility. The exact role and function of the EBA changed over time following its founding in 1902. By November 1918, membership in the association was mandatory for most classes of BRT blue-collar workers; dues were 50 cents per month—an hour's wage for a veteran motorman and almost two hours' wage for an entry-level worker (see Table 3).[2]

BRT management opposed independent trade unions for the usual reasons cited by industrial managers in the early 20th century.

TABLE 3: HOURLY WAGES FOR BRT TRANSIT WORKERS, JULY 26, 1918

Years of Service	Guard	Conductor	Motorman
1	$0.26	$0.31	$0.40
2	.27	.32	.41
3	.28	.33	.42
4	.29	.34	.43
5	.29	.35	.48
6 or more	.29	.35	.50

Source: Data compiled from BRT Monthly (August 1918).

They claimed that powerful and independent unions would drive up costs and were examples of rampant Bolshevism unleashed in their midst.[3] Moreover, the fact that the EBA relieved the BRT from the need to incorporate a range of employee benefits into its own cost and pay structure was an even more practical reason for holding off organizers from independent trade and craft unions.

In 1916, the Brotherhood of Locomotive Engineers decided that a fresh effort was needed to organize BRT motormen. In June 1918, W. J. Orr established a second local chapter for BRT workers, Local No. 868. The new local complemented Local No. 419, which dated back to the days of steam locomotives on the elevated trains. The older chapter, headquartered in Penn-Fulton Hall, largely served workers in the BRT's eastern division, routes such as the Fulton Street elevated line which operated out of the company's yards and shops in the East New York section of Brooklyn. The new local was set up in Prospect Hall; its base of workers was from the BRT's southern division, which included elevated lines that operated out of the 36th Street yards and shop. The potential membership for this new local also included workers on the former excursion railways to and from Coney Island that had been absorbed into the BRT at the turn of the century.

As Orr's membership drive began to bear fruit during the summer of 1918, the BRT's response was to discharge 40 or more motormen, approximately 10 percent of its total force of such workers.[4] Each firing was nominally for some specific failure to observe the BRT's rules and regulations. However, a reasonably independent review board determined that in at least 29 of 40 cases, the company's actions were motivated solely by its belief that the men were sympathetic to the union's membership drive.

The union's first reaction to the wholesale firing was to call an immediate strike; the walkout was set for August 7, 1918. But the union delayed its action and instead agreed to submit its grievance to a new federal panel, the National War Labor Board, which had been established the previous year by presidential proclamation to help ensure labor-management harmony to support the country's war effort.

The War Labor Board quickly agreed to hear the case. On five separate days—August 13, 14, 15, 20, and 21—hearings were held in the Post Office Building, which stood in what is today City Hall Park in lower Manhattan. BRT management denied that there was any dispute over which the War Labor Board had jurisdiction. "No controversy existed in this case between employers and workers at the time the War Labor Board instituted an inquiry," claimed BRT President Timothy Williams.[5]

Having registered their objection formally and for the record, management representatives participated in the hearings, gave testimony, and responded to inquiries posed by the War Labor Board staff. The BRT team who appeared before the board was led by vice president John J. Dempsey and general counsel George D. Yoemans.[6]

These August meetings were business-like working sessions; a formal record was established that would be the basis for later decision making when the board conducted closed-door deliberations on the brotherhood's petition. Each firing was examined individually and in detail during these meetings.[7]

On September 19, 1918, a different style of hearing was held. The two appointed members of the War Labor Board, former U.S. President William Howard Taft and a man by the name of Frank P. Walsh, presided over these hearings. Testimony was forthcoming from various local political eminences, and participants were free to put forth ideology and opinion in abundance on subjects often having little to do with the firings. New York Mayor John F. Hylan, for example, advanced his strong feelings that under no circumstances should the BRT be allowed to use the dispute as justification for increasing transit fares.[8] Mayor Hylan regarded none of his political adversaries with quite the passion he reserved for the private companies that operated rapid transit service in New York—the Interborough Rapid Transit Company and the BRT.

In late October the War Labor Board issued its report. The board found that in 29 of the 40 cases the workers had been discharged solely because of their association with the Brotherhood of Locomotive Engineers and that, furthermore, such action was a violation of President Woodrow Wilson's proclamation in establishing the War Labor Board. In its formal report, the War Labor Board issued the following statement:

> We are brought to this conclusion primarily by the admissions of the President of the company and other high officials as to their attitude of opposition to the men joining the unions chosen by them as most desirable for their welfare, by the espionage of the officials of the company in the neighborhood of the meeting place of the organization and elsewhere, by the fact that the dismissals were abnormally large in number during the two months when the issue as to the unions was acute, as compared with dismissals for years prior to that time.[9]

The report recommended that the BRT rehire the men and award back pay from the time the workers were discharged. However, the War Labor Board could only recommend; in the case of the Brotherhood of Locomotive Engineers versus New York Consolidated Railroad Company (that is, the BRT), the board lacked statutory authority to enforce its findings.

The War Labor Board issued its report in Washington, D.C., on Thursday, October 24, 1918. No one knew it at the time, of course, but this action started the clock ticking on the final countdown to the Malbone Street Wreck eight days later. For a day or so, BRT officials could rightly claim that they had not yet received a formal copy of the report or had not yet had a chance to give the document the careful review it deserved. "I haven't seen the official text of the decision yet and I would rather not discuss it until I do," BRT president Williams told the press on Friday morning, October 25.[10]

The Brotherhood of Locomotive Engineers was elated. "The result is a victory for organized labor," said George W. Martin, an attorney speaking for W. J. Orr.[11] But by early the following week, the union was beginning to get edgy.

On Tuesday, October 29, a three-man delegation of BRT workers, acting on behalf of the brotherhood, called on vice president Dempsey at BRT headquarters, 85 Clinton Street in Brooklyn, to discuss the War Labor Board's report. Dempsey was unable to see them, but an appointment was made for 11:00 A.M. the following day. The men returned and Dempsey, after keeping them waiting for almost an hour, said that he would not see them as a group. The BRT was unwilling to grant even tacit recognition to the union; Dempsey, undoubtedly after frantic conversations with other BRT executives during the time the trio cooled their heels outside his office, concluded that meeting with the men collectively would concede the point. Dempsey said he was willing to meet with each of the three individually, as BRT workers, but the men refused this offer and reported back to the union.

By this time, the BRT had reached a decision as to what to do about the findings of the War Labor Board. As outlined in Dempsey's October 29 letter to the elected trustees of the EBA on behalf of BRT management, the company asked the EBA to review the report of the War Labor Board and forward appropriate recommendations. In his letter to the trustees, Dempsey said the company would honor whatever the EBA recommended, including rehiring discharged employees and awarding back pay. Attached to Dempsey's letter was a "statement of principle" about labor relations in general that was taken from testimony Williams had given before the War Labor Board on September 19.[12] In the light of the company's past position with respect to the authority of the War Labor Board and the firings themselves, it is certainly possible to read a note of conciliation into this action; the BRT had earlier denied not only the War Labor Board's jurisdiction, but even the fact that there was any dispute in need of resolution. Now it was seemingly ready to accept the board's recommendations.

But whether this action was conciliatory or otherwise, the brotherhood's reaction to it was one of sheer fury. The despised "company union" had been introduced into a dispute that the brotherhood alone had carried to the War Labor Board, and that the brotherhood firmly believed was a bilateral matter between the Brotherhood of Locomotive Engineers and the BRT. Furthermore, the brotherhood believed it had emerged victorious by virtue of the board's final report and recommendation—clearly a victory on the short-term issue of the mass firing and perhaps even the first step of a longer-term victory of formal recognition by management. In response to the BRT's introducing the EBA into the dispute, the Brotherhood of Locomotive Engineers called on its members among the company's motormen and motor-switchmen to walk off the job at 5:00 A.M. on Friday, November 1, 1918. They did.

Throughout the day on November 1, both sides debated about how disruptive of normal BRT rapid transit service the strike proved to be. The union claimed that 80 percent of the company's motormen and motor-switchmen had walked off the job; the BRT spoke of minor inconveniences as it rushed into service as motormen a number of other employees who had received rudimentary training over the previous weeks in anticipation of some such turn of events. The best guess is that of about 450 regular motormen and motor-switchmen who were scheduled to work on the average weekday, 200 or so honored the strike. While replacements were found for many of these men, one certainty is that BRT passengers were inconvenienced by the action and the morning rush hour on November 1 was anything but normal.[13]

It was this inconvenience—or, more precisely, the failure of the BRT to operate acceptable levels of rapid transit service as called for under the terms of the Dual Subway Contracts—that introduced yet another player to the whole business. The New York State Public Service Commission for the First District (the PSC) had no jurisdiction over a dispute between a labor union and the BRT. But the PSC could and did step in when it became apparent on November 1 that adequate mass transit service was not being provided by the BRT under the terms of the Dual Subway Contracts, which the PSC was responsible for enforcing and monitoring.[14]

At the direction of its chairman, Charles Bulkley Hubbell, the PSC called both sides to its New York headquarters at 29 Lafayette Street in Manhattan. Because the BRT was still maintaining the position that it did not recognize the Brotherhood of Locomotive Engineers as a representative of its workers, the PSC put each side in a separate room and began the slow and painful task of mediating a labor-management dispute, a process that was not at all aided by the fact one sided refused to admit the other's legitimacy.[15]

After preliminary meetings earlier on November 1, more serious sessions got under way toward evening. Representing the BRT were John Dempsey and Timothy Williams; the Brotherhood of Locomotive Engineers sent L. G. Griffing, W. J. Orr, and seven other union officials to the meeting. As the mediation continued into the evening with little to show for the effort, word reached 29 Lafayette

Street of a terrible accident on the BRT's Brighton Beach Line in Brooklyn near Prospect Park with large numbers of casualties. Principals of both the BRT and the PSC left immediately for the scene. BRT vice president John Dempsey, not feeling well throughout the day, collapsed at the news. A PSC doctor insisted he go home immediately and leave the day's unfinished business to others.

As the full scope of the disaster began to unfold, BRT and brotherhood representatives back at Lafayette Street narrowed their differences in quantum leaps. At 1:45 A.M., they reached full agreement on all matters; it took another hour or so to have the agreement typed up and signed, with the BRT, the Brotherhood of Locomotive Engineers, and the PSC being signatories to the document.[16]

All of the 29 fired workers would be reinstated with back pay, and the cases of the other 11—whose dismissals the War Labor Board found either to be perfectly proper or without sufficient evidence for a finding—would be given a fresh review. The strike was over, and full service would be restored in time for Saturday morning's rush hour on BRT lines—that is, on all lines except the Brighton Beach Line. Operations would not be back to normal there until Monday morning, November 4. On the other hand, it is also perfectly correct to say that after the strike of November 1, 1918, things never got back to normal on the BRT's Brighton Beach Line.

NOTES

1. The BRT preferred the single-e spelling of the word *employees*. For information about the EBA, although very much from the perspective of BRT management, see H. A. Bullock, "Employes' [sic] Benefit Association," *BRT Monthly* (January 1916), 3–5. See also "The Brooklyn Rapid Transit Employee's Benefit Association—Some Interesting Features Concerning Its Organization and Methods of Work," *Street Railway Journal* 20 (December 13, 1902), 950–51.

2. *BRT Monthly* (August 1918), 4.

3. The BRT's company magazine often contained little epigrams and short articles equating trade unionism with Bolshevism. See, for example, "Ole Hanson on Bolshevism," *BRT Monthly* (November–December 1919), 8.

4. *New York Times* (July 16, 1918), 6.

5. "Excerpts from Statement Made by President T. S. Williams to the National War Labor Board at a Hearing on Labor Union Matters, City Hall, September 19, 1918."

6. *New York Times* (August 16, 1918), 7.

7. A lengthy file of the National War Labor Board's work in the case, including verbatim transcripts of all hearings and staff recommendations on which the board's final actions were based, may be found in the National Archives. See National War Labor Board, "The Brotherhood of Locomotive Engineers vs. The New York Consolidated Railway *(sic)* Company" (1918), docket 283, National Archives, Suitland, Md.

8. Ibid., page 13 of the hearing transcript for September 19, 1918.

9. National War Labor Board, "Findings in Re Brotherhood of Locomotive Engineers vs. New York Consolidated Railroad Company" (1918), docket 283, National Archives, Suitland, Md. For a news account, see *New York Times* (October 25, 1918), 11.

10. *Brooklyn Eagle* (October 25, 1918), 3.

11. Ibid.

12. For the text of Dempsey's letter, including Williams's statement, see *BRT Monthly* (November 1918): 2–3.

13. The *Brooklyn Eagle* (November 1, 1918), 1, reported the percentage of regular service that was operating on various BRT rapid transit lines in midmorning on November 1, 1918, as follows: Brighton Beach Line, 80 to 85 percent; Lexington Avenue Line, 75 percent; Fulton Street Line, 75 percent; Fifth Avenue and Culver lines, 100 percent; West End and Sea Beach lines, 75 percent; Fourth Avenue subway, 100 percent; Broadway subway, 80 percent; Ridgewood (Myrtle Avenue) Line, 50 percent. The PSC estimated that, overall, between 50 and 75 percent of regular rapid transit service operated over BRT lines on November 1, 1918; this is roughly consistent with the newspaper estimates cited above. See Public Service Commission for the First District, *Report for the Year Ending December 31, 1918* (Albany, N.Y.: J. B. Lyon Company, 1919), 1:142–8.

14. Public Service Commission, *Report*, 1: 142–8.

15. Ibid.

16. For the text of the agreement, see "BRT Strike Is Declared Ended," *New York Journal* (November 2, 1918), 5. For further information on the agreement, see Public Service Commission, *Report*, 1:142–6.

CHAPTER 4
The Motorman

When a 25-year-old man who was known to his colleagues at the Brooklyn Rapid Transit Company (the BRT) as Billy Lewis left home for work on Friday, November 1, 1918, it was close to four o'clock in the morning and the sky over New York was still pitch black. Somewhere out over the Atlantic Ocean, daylight was racing westward to bring another sunrise to the North American coastline. When daylight later departed into the west and returned Brooklyn to a state of darkness, the night became as bleak and gruesome as the borough would ever know.

Lewis lived in Brooklyn at 160 34th Street in a four-story apartment house adjacent to the new Bush Terminal. His was typical of smart, new residential construction going up along the route of the BRT's new Fourth Avenue subway, a principal element of the transit network the company was awarded during the negotiation of the Dual Subway Contracts in 1913.[1] The 36th Street express station on the Fourth Avenue subway was a short walk from Lewis's home. Also nearby was the BRT's complex at 36th Street and Fifth Avenue where the company maintained its rapid transit cars and trains. As a young man intending to make his career with the BRT, Lewis had selected a convenient neighborhood in which to live.

Tragedy had recently struck young Lewis's family, though. Two weeks earlier, his three-year-old daughter Genevieve had fallen ill with the Spanish influenza that ultimately claimed the lives of more than a half-million Americans. It was over quickly; never a robust child, she died quietly at home on Friday, October 25, and was buried in Holy Cross Cemetery in Brooklyn on Tuesday, October 29, three days before the Malbone Street Wreck. Within a few more days, 12 victims of that accident would also be laid to rest in Holy Cross.

This was not the first time that Lewis and his wife Josephine had buried a child. Four years earlier another daughter, one-year-old Frances, had passed away. As Billy Lewis headed for work on November 1, 1918, he carried the sad realization that, of three children born to him and his wife, only one was still alive—a year-old girl named Geraldine.

There was something else about the recent death of little Genevieve. A week before she died of influenza, Lewis himself had taken ill with the same dreaded disease. He was lucky; he recovered. But this series of events raises a troubling question: What was the state of Billy Lewis's mind on November 1, 1918? He himself had been ill, his daughter had just died, and it is likely that he regarded himself as the carrier of the disease that claimed his daughter's life. This issue is important because before November 1 was over, Billy Lewis—a dispatcher for the BRT—was given an emergency assignment as a motorman to help offset the effects of the strike called for that day by the Brotherhood of Locomotive Engineers. At 6:42 P.M., dispatcher-turned-motorman Billy Lewis was in the cab operating the train that was involved in the Malbone Street Wreck.

Except the man's real name was not Billy Lewis. His name was Edward Luciano. It is reasonable to suggest that he identified himself as Lewis in an effort to avoid the virulent anti-Italian bias prevalent in New York at the time.[2] For the remainder of this account, the man will be identified by his authentic surname.

On November 1, 1918, Luciano's regular assignment with the BRT was in the company's Culver Depot at West Fifth Street and Surf Avenue in Coney Island, operational headquarters for both the Brighton Beach Line and the Culver Line. He was a crew dispatcher on the day trick, having been promoted from the night trick in July 1918. The 25-year-old Luciano had joined the BRT in 1916 as a guard aboard the company's elevated trains. He also had worked as an operator in a switch tower and as a train dispatcher during his short career with the company.

Although Brighton Beach and Culver Line services were coordinated and supervised out of Culver Depot in Coney Island, and although Brighton Beach Line trains had begun using Culver Depot as their southern terminal in 1903 when service was extended beyond the original terminal adjacent to the Brighton Beach Hotel, on November 1, 1918, Culver Depot was not the southern terminal for Brighton Beach Line trains. To allow construction of a new BRT Coney Island terminal at Surf and Stillwell avenues as called for under the Dual Subway Contracts plus an elevated line parallel to the oceanfront between the new terminal and Brighton Beach, in 1916 Brighton Beach Line trains were temporarily cut back to Sheepshead Bay to facilitate work on the project.

By November 1, 1918, much of this new construction was already in place. On October 21, 1918, Brighton Beach Line trains began using a new elevated station in Brighton Beach, and various shuttle trains were running between Brighton Beach and Coney Island. Basic Brighton Beach Line service, though, was using Brighton Beach as its southern terminal on November 1, and Culver Depot was operating not only in its final months but in the shadow, quite literally, of the new elevated structure that would soon give BRT trains access to the Coney Island terminal that would open for revenue service on May 29, 1919. Culver Depot, a marvelous three-story wooden structure with numerous dormer windows that was built by Andrew Culver in 1873 for steam-powered trains of his Prospect Park and Coney Island Railroad and that survived to become an oceanfront terminal served by BRT elevated trains and trolley cars in the early era of electric transportation, was demolished in 1922.[3]

Luciano's title, crew dispatcher, may have a supervisory ring to it. His actual tasks, however, were more clerical than managerial. He checked train operating personnel in and out and recorded their comings and goings on large sheets of paper. He was, for all intents and purposes, a clerk, but he was looking forward to his next advancement up the BRT career ladder.

A typical sequence on the BRT's lines involved entry-level employment as a guard; next might come the position of conductor. Both of these positions involved working aboard trains in regular passenger service, but performing such functions as opening and closing doors or gates at stations—not operating the train. Next, assignment to a position such as crew dispatcher or tower operator was common, followed by advancement to the position of motor-switchman—a job that called for the operation of trains, but only in and around yards and terminals with no passengers aboard. Finally one advanced to motorman, the key person within the operating ranks; the motorman, who operated trains in revenue passenger service, was at the top of the ladder with respect to rate of pay.[4] (In 1918, the term *motorman* was perfectly correct; there were no women operating BRT trains, although wartime pressures did see hundreds of women join the company's ranks as guards and conductors.)

Earlier in 1918, Luciano had supposedly begun training for advancement to the rank of motor-switchman; he was given two and a half hours of formal classroom instruction, but, for one reason or another, his training was not continued. Then in the fall, when the brotherhood's strike began to loom, the company sent Luciano out over the road with regular motormen for some practical experience in train operations. This series of events raises the next question, one that is very important to an understanding of the Malbone Street Wreck: What was the extent and nature of Edward Luciano's experience and training in the operation of rapid transit trains on November 1, 1918?

The BRT's protocol for instructing its motormen and motor-switchmen was detailed and explicit. First came a physical examination. Next was a 60-hour course, taught by a qualified instructor to small groups of five or six men at a time. After completing the course, candidates had to pass a 90-question examination. If successful, they were then sent to a division superintendent for the next phase of training, apprenticeship aboard regular trains in the company of a fully qualified motorman for another 60 hours, including at least three days on each line or route in the superintendent's jurisdiction. Testing and certification of candidates was mandatory after this apprenticeship.[5] Assuming a trainee successfully passed all requisite examinations, turning a green recruit into a qualified motorman involved a minimum of 120 hours of instruction and training. Once qualified, a new motorman could only expect to work around yards and terminals as a motor-switchman until he gained even more experience.

No BRT instructor or other company official ever subjected Edward Luciano to any kind of review of his qualifications to serve as a motorman. Apparently Luciano did not even undergo the routine physical examination that was normally the very first evaluation the company required of individuals who wished to operate its trains. The company's inattention to Luciano's evaluation raises the possibility that the two and a half hours of classroom instruction he had received earlier in 1918 was not part of a career advancement to motorman at all, but rather a brief orientation into the work of a motorman that he would need to know for his own duties as a crew dispatcher. The full extent of Luciano's formal training as a motorman was that brief classroom instruction plus two days of riding in the cab with regular motormen immediately before the strike. Luciano's over-the-road training, brief as it was, involved no work on the Brighton Beach Line. It was restricted to the BRT's Culver Line and Fifth Avenue Line.[6]

Operating an electric rapid transit train demands specialized skills that are unlike those required to operate other kinds of complex machinery. Although the skills are not overly difficult to acquire— the "washout" rate among candidates does not rival that of fighter pilots or professional football players—their absence can result in disaster. Acquiring those skills was all the more important on the BRT's electrified elevated lines in 1918, because there were fewer built-in mechanical safeguards to compensate for human error than there are today.

With respect to train operation, mastery of the braking system was the truly vital function. It is relatively simple to feed electric current to a train's motors and make it go; stopping the train smoothly, and exactly when and where one wants it to stop, takes some skill. Such skill comes only from experience. One can develop some rudimentary understanding of the braking system used on BRT elevated trains in 1918 by contrasting it with the brakes found on automobiles today. In an automobile, the hydraulic braking system sees its maximum pressure during the application of the brakes. Further, if the brake lines should rupture while an automobile is moving, the brakes are lost and one is in trouble.

In very simplified terms, on a train the air brake system is at maximum pressure in order to release the brakes and allow the train to move. If a train's main brake line should rupture while the train is under way, the brakes are applied and the train stops. With an automobile, "no brakes" means one cannot stop the vehicle; with a train, "no brakes" usually means the vehicle cannot move. The actual physical force of applying train brakes comes from positive air pressure that is held in tanks in each car, but the brakes on each car are controlled from the head end by variations in air pressure in a main brake line that runs from car to car. A measured reduction of pressure in this brake line produces a proportionate brake application, while a massive reduction produces a full emergency application.[7] This is still the way brakes function on most railroad trains; contemporary braking on subway trains has evolved into slightly more complicated electropneumatic systems.

Another difference between the braking systems on trains and automobiles involves timing. In an automobile, one applies the brakes and braking action is immediate and direct. Furthermore, one is in continuous contact with the braking system through the brake pedal, and instantaneous corrections in pressure can be made in response to changing conditions. With train brakes, on the other hand, there is a delay between application and action. On a moving train, when the motorman makes a brake application, he reduces air pressure in the main brake line; this sends a signal to the braking apparatus aboard each car that causes the steel brake shoes to come into contact with the rolling surface of the car's wheels. But it takes many seconds—on a long and fast-moving railroad freight train, it can even be a matter of minutes—for the process to register its full effect. The motorman's ability to anticipate the need for braking action is critical; this ability can only be gained through experience and knowledge—experience with the way the brakes respond and knowledge of conditions ahead.

Luciano had been given some apprentice-style training in elevated train operations prior to November 1, 1918. It was not, however, in anticipation of routine advancement to the position of motorswitchman. Rather it was an emergency action to expand the pool of workers the BRT could draw from to operate revenue passenger trains should a strike materialize.

Two potentially mitigating circumstances must be noted. The first was the recent death of Luciano's daughter, which could well have affected the man's state of mind and his ability to concentrate. He was sent out for this road training immediately upon returning to work after her funeral. Second, it was eminently clear in late October 1918 that the BRT was attempting to gear itself up to conduct business in the event of a strike. Regular motormen who were normally helpful and encouraging to the company's trainees may very well have been less helpful, if not downright hostile to the new trainees. They may have realized that the trainees were being prepared to help the company survive an action by a union with which they sympathized. Indeed, they may have held union membership and may have planned to honor the pending strike.

Luciano began his day's work as a crew dispatcher in Culver Depot at 5:00 A.M. on November 1, the very hour the strike began. He was to go off duty eleven and a half hours later at 4:30 P.M.; because of the strike and a need to make all manner of unusual crew assignments to fill in for striking motormen, the day must have been as hectic as it was long. Throughout the day, Luciano would have interacted with the BRT's senior officer in Culver Depot—William Brody, a 14-year veteran employee who bore the title of trainmaster. (Brody must not be confused with Charles A. Boody, a member of the board of directors of the New York Consolidated Railroad, the BRT subsidiary that operated its rapid transit trains.) Throughout the day, Brody made a series of ad hoc assignments to compensate for the many regular motormen who were observing the strike. Any number of clerks, towermen, maintenance workers, conductors, and company security officers who had received rudimentary motorman's training in late October were sent out on November 1 in the cabs of Brighton Beach and Culver Line elevated trains. All received a bonus from the BRT of $20 and a promise of a permanent increase in pay once the strike was over. As crew dispatcher, Edward Luciano was the man who recorded all these assignments at Culver Depot.

Brody's immediate contact with the BRT chain of command was Thomas F. Blewitt, superintendent of rapid transit operations for the BRT's southern division. Blewitt's office was located in the company's 36th Street complex, a short distance from Luciano's home. Once the press of the morning rush hour was over, Blewitt and Brody began to make plans for handling the evening rush hour, from approximately 4:30 to 7:00 P.M., when the city's workforce headed home for supper and relaxation.

As the day wore on, it appeared that Blewitt and Brody had their bases covered for the evening rush hour. They were able to find a patchwork force to fill in for striking motormen on the Brighton Beach and Culver lines. One piece of work, though, remained unassigned. Brody and Blewitt needed one final motorman for a single trip from the Kings Highway station on the Culver Line across to Manhattan via the Fifth Avenue elevated line and the Brooklyn Bridge, then back to Brighton Beach over the Fulton Street elevated and the Brighton Beach Line; the distance was 20 miles, and the running time was an hour and 40 minutes.

Here is where subsequent accounts, including sworn testimony, fail to tell a consistent story. Did Luciano simply volunteer for the assignment upon realizing it was available or did Brody seek him out? Was Luciano talked into doing something that he might otherwise have felt unqualified to do? Did Luciano talk Brody into giving him the assignment or was he simply ordered to take out the train? A case can be made for any of these possibilities on the basis of what was later said. What remains an incontestable fact, however, is that Luciano wound up in the motorman's cab and the BRT's normal safeguards for keeping unqualified personnel out of harm's way utterly failed to work.

As superintendent, Blewitt was the man who normally made the final decision that a trainee was properly qualified to serve as a motorman over the routes in his division. He reviewed a man's training and apprenticeship and, if everything was in order, he put a final signature on the documentation that made it all official. In a way, Blewitt played a shadow version of his regular role under the emergency conditions brought on by the strike. During a late-afternoon telephone conversation between Brody and Blewitt—with Luciano present in Brody's office at Culver Depot—Blewitt supposedly told Brody that Luciano was a properly qualified motorman.[8]

This was not a careful and professional judgment Blewitt made back in his office at 36th Street after closely reviewing Luciano's personnel file. Nor was it anything at all like the final judgment Blewitt normally made about candidates who had successfully completed the company's regular training program. It was more like an exasperated shrug that said, in effect, individuals with similar qualifications had been sent out over the road as substitute motormen all day, so why not take one more chance with this man. Luciano was not a "qualified motorman," and no amount of saying so could ever make it so. On the other hand, if finding anyone who had even the slightest knowledge of how to operate an elevated train was the extent to which the railway's own standards had fallen because of the strike, then Blewitt was saying that even Luciano could be called a "qualified motorman." It was a decision that would soon bring death to at least 93 people; it would also result in the indictment of Thomas Blewitt for manslaughter.

In retrospect, Brody, Blewitt, and Luciano probably had enough information among themselves to realize that the decision was a bad one, even by the relaxed standards that were unofficially prevailing during the strike. But the various pieces of information they each possessed were not properly drawn out in conversation as the decision was reached. It is unlikely, for example, that either Brody or

Blewitt would have sanctioned Luciano for the assignment if they realized that he had never been over the Brighton Beach Line in the cab of a train, or that his minimal hands-on operating experience took place immediately after the death of his daughter. But everyone was in too much of a hurry—Brody and Blewitt because they wanted to keep the railroad running, Luciano because he could use the extra money and was eager to advance his career at the BRT.

Edward Luciano, with minimal skills in train operation, was sent out to operate a rush-hour train in the dark of night over a Brighton Beach Line that he had never before seen from the cab of a train and whose alignment at one critical spot had recently been significantly changed. Brody later claimed he gave Luciano a special warning about the new construction at Prospect Park. If he did, it was an admonition that Luciano failed to comprehend. On the basis of faulty assumptions and a perfectly understandable desire to keep the trains rolling, the BRT awkwardly, tragically, and stupidly stumbled into the worst mistake in the history of American urban transportation. (See appendix A for a comparison of death statistics associated with the Malbone Street Wreck and fatal casualties associated with other disasters.)

NOTES

1. Construction of the Fourth Avenue subway was begun even before the Dual Subway Contracts and was assigned to the BRT during the negotiation of the contracts.

2. *BRT Monthly* (March 1917): 12.

3. For information on Culver Depot, see "An Improved Terminal for Handling the Heavy Coney Island Crowds—Brooklyn Rapid Transit Company," *Street Railway Journal* 23 (June 11, 1904): 884–8; "Culver Terminal, Relic of Idealists' Dream," *BRT Monthly* (July 1919): 3; "Culver Terminal, at Coney Island, Is Torn Down," *BRT Monthly* (January 1923): 4.

4. See chapter 3, table 3, for prevailing rates of pay for various positions on the BRT.

5. During the criminal and civil trials following the Malbone Street Wreck, the BRT avoided producing any formal company documents that specified the details of its training and qualification procedures for motormen. Earlier articles document the degree of seriousness, if not the precise procedures, the company believed was required in this area. See, for exam-

ple, "A Motorman's School System in Brooklyn," *Street Railway Journal* 25 (1905): 1056–63. While this deals with the training of motormen for street-cars, not rapid transit trains, it is very descriptive and includes copies of the examinations candidates were required to pass. Furthermore, because BRT streetcars often operated over rapid transit tracks en route to Coney Island, streetcar and rapid transit training shared certain commonalities. For other insights into rapid transit training, see "New Instruction Car for the Brooklyn Rapid Transit Company," *Street Railway Journal* 26 (1906): 162–5. See also, "BRT Surface School Room," *BRT Monthly* (March 1917): 4–6, 17. Further discussion of the company's testing and qualification procedures took place during one of the later trials. See *Brooklyn Times* (March 6, 1919), 1–2; and *Brooklyn Times* (March 12, 1919), 1.

6. Following the Malbone Street Wreck, various individuals offered widely different versions of the extent of Luciano's experience, some even suggesting that he had operated over the Brighton Beach Line. See, for example, *Brooklyn Times* (March 6, 1919), 1. The preponderance of information, however, suggests that Luciano's experience was limited to the Culver and Fifth Avenue lines.

7. A device aboard each car called a triple valve is the critical piece of equipment that responds to changes in air pressure in the main brake line and initiates brake applications.

8. Benjamin Brody later testified that Blewitt said of Luciano: "Use him; he's a qualified motorman." See *Brooklyn Eagle* (November 8, 1918), 2.

After the tragic Malbone Street Wreck of 1918, the thoroughfare was renamed Empire Boulevard to avoid association with the accident. However,
the name Malbone Street is still used in Brooklyn to designate a short dead-
end street near the site of the infamous disaster. (*Author*)

The Prospect Park Station on the BRT's Brighton Beach Line before it was rebuilt to its present configuration. The top photo looks south toward Brighton Beach and shows the trolley car loop where passengers could transfer to and from elevated trains on the lower level. The lower photo looks west; Brighton Beach Line trains operated below grade inside the stone-lined cut. At left is the former Hotel Melrose; the building on the right is the former Prospect Park Depot of the Brooklyn, Flatbush and Coney Island Railroad. (*Collection of Donald W. Harold*)

The Prospect Park Station as it looks today. The accident occurred in the tunnel at left. The train on the right is a shuttle about to depart for Franklin Avenue. Center tracks are used by trains heading to and from DeKalb Avenue. Luciano's fatal train would have paused on the track at the far left. (*Author*)

Looking south from Washington Avenue, toward the fatal tunnel. The crossover switch tracks were not in place in 1918. (*Author*)

This tower at Franklin and Fulton controlled the junction where the Brighton Beach Line diverged from the Fulton Street Line. (*Collection of Donald W. Harold*)

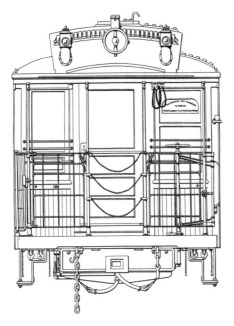

An outline drawing of a typical BRT elevated car. (*Author's collection*)

The entrance to the Malbone Street tunnel the day after the tragic accident. Note markings on the face of the tunnel, caused when the derailed train smashed into it. (*Collection of Donald W. Harold*)

A view of the wrecked train inside the tunnel. (*Collection of Donald W. Harold*)

A worker stands atop the wreckage of BRT el car No. 100 inside the Malbone Street tunnel. (*Collection of Donald W. Harold*)

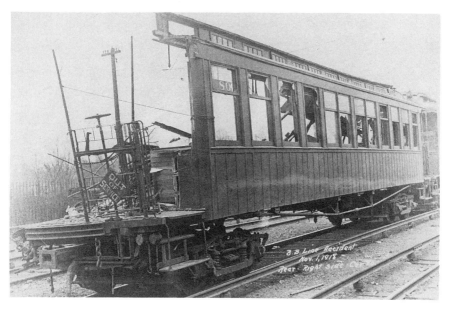

BRT el car No. 80 at the 36th Street Yard days after the accident. This car was never returned to service. (*Collection of Donald W. Harold*)

Rear end of the train inside the Malbone Street tunnel. This is car No. 1064, which was the lead car on the trip from Kings Highway to Park Row. (*Collection of Donald W. Harold*)

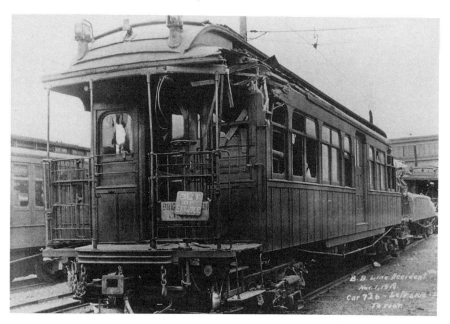

Car No. 726, the lead car of the fatal train, shown at the 36th Street Yard days after the accident. Motorman Luciano operated the train from inside a small cab located behind the car's end platform. (*Collection of Donald W. Harold*)

CHAPTER 5

The Accident

After Brody and Blewitt agreed that Luciano could fill in as a temporary motorman to round out their personnel assignments for the evening rush hour, Brody took Luciano to a small, two-track yard immediately south of the Kings Highway station on the BRT's Culver Line. The yard originally served as a terminal for special trains carrying passengers, in season, to an adjacent racetrack of the Brooklyn Jockey Association, one of three such facilities served by the early Coney Island–bound excursion railways.[1] Horse racing ended in Brooklyn in 1909, and the small terminal was converted into a train storage yard. Today the site of the old terminal and yard is a city playground where Brooklyn youngsters sharpen their basketball skills and their elders enjoy a few sets of tennis.

Those familiar with the Culver Line today think immediately of a heavy-duty rapid transit line served by the F train and operating on a three-track elevated structure above McDonald Avenue in Brooklyn. On November 1, 1918, the line was different, although it was about to change. Today's elevated structure is a product of the Dual Subway Contracts; although it was largely in place on the day of the Malbone Street Wreck, it was not in service and would not be until early 1919. Instead, BRT elevated trains were then operating in much the same manner as did excursion trains on Andrew Culver's Prospect Park and Coney Island Railroad in the 1870s; they made use of tracks that ran along the surface on a right-of-way in the middle of the street—a street that in 1918 was not called McDonald Avenue, as it is today, but Gravesend Avenue.

Culver Line "elevated" trains ran along the same tracks as Gravesend Avenue trolley cars, and motormen had to be mindful of street traffic at intersections. As was standard safety practice under such circumstances, trains drew their electric current from an overhead trolley wire, not a track-level third rail.

In 1918 the Prospect Park and Coney Island Railroad no longer terminated, excursion-railway style, on the periphery of Brooklyn's downtown district at Ninth Avenue and 20th Street on the northeast side of Greenwood Cemetery. Instead, trains proceeded to the southwest corner of the cemetery and there ascended a ramp and became part of the BRT elevated system over the Fifth Avenue Line.[2]

The Fifth Avenue Line had been built as part of the Brooklyn Elevated/Union Elevated rapid transit system between 1888 and 1890. In addition to being an important elevated line that linked downtown Brooklyn and residential neighborhoods in Bay Ridge, it provided three of the one-time Coney Island excursion railways—the Brooklyn, Bath and West End; the New York and Sea Beach; and the Prospect Park and Coney Island—the opportunity to operate trains into downtown Brooklyn. The Fifth Avenue Line did for these three excursion railways what the Fulton Street elevated did for the Brighton Beach Line. By 1918, of course, the Fifth Avenue Line had become part of the overall BRT system.

Thus, not only did the Culver Line trains have access to the business district of downtown Brooklyn via the Fifth Avenue Line but, because the Fifth Avenue elevated connected with the Myrtle Avenue Line, they could make their way across the Brooklyn Bridge to the Park Row elevated terminal in Manhattan. Park Row was also a terminal for the Brighton Beach Line, and so the following service pattern of the train to which Luciano was assigned was possible: Kings Highway to Park Row over the Culver, Fifth Avenue, and Myrtle Avenue lines, then back to Brooklyn over the Fulton Street and Brighton Beach lines (see map 2).

Luciano was given a set of control handles and keys, the ordinary working tools of a BRT motorman. It is unlikely that he was wearing the striped coveralls, matching jacket, and black peaked cap of a regular motorman, and his status as an irregular in the cab was probably marked by his ordinary attire. When he got to the yard at Kings Highway, Luciano met up with the four men who would be his train crew. Such a seemingly large complement was needed for a five-car train because of the way BRT elevated cars were designed. In imitation of conventional railroad equipment of the late-19th century, elevated cars were boarded by way of porch-like platforms at each end of the car. These open platforms, so-called, were protected by an overhang of the car's roof, but were otherwise exposed to the elements. Once aboard the platform, passengers turned and entered the body of the car through sliding doors in the end bulkheads. The

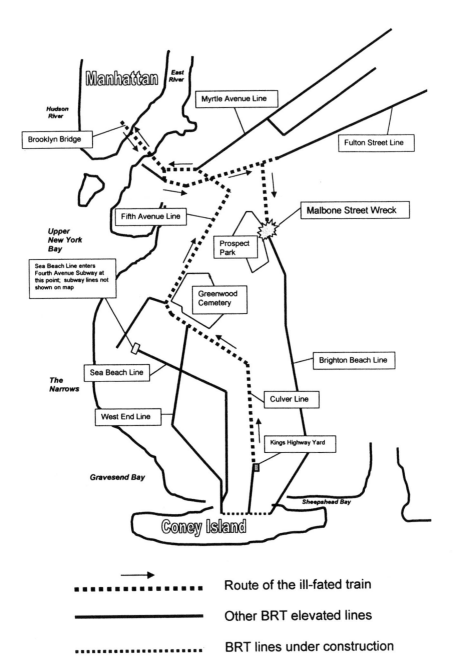

···→···	Route of the ill-fated train
———	Other BRT elevated lines
············	BRT lines under construction

open platforms had gates along their sides, and it was the manual operation of these gates at stations that required stationing a separate crew member at the point where cars were coupled together to open and close the gates, oversee the boarding of passengers, and signal the motorman with a bell-cord system when station work was completed. The gates on BRT elevated cars were not mechanically or electrically interlocked to prevent a train's moving when the gates were open, as are subway car doors today.

The platforms at the front and the rear of a train were off limits to passengers, and the following warning was posted on each platform of every BRT elevated car: "Passengers Are Forbidden to Ride on Front or Rear Platforms of Trains." A five-car train required four uniformed crew members, one assigned to the post between the first and second car, another between the second and third, and so forth. Plus, of course, the motorman.

Conductor Michael Turner was stationed between the first and second cars, and the other three crew members bore the lesser title of guard. One of them—48-year-old Morris Weinberg, assigned to the post between the second and third cars—would later in the evening become the only BRT employee to be killed in the Malbone Street Wreck.[3]

Luciano operated the train from a small, enclosed motorman's cab inside the lead car on the right side facing forward. "Inside" the car means that the motorman's control station was behind the open platform at the front of the train. What is still not known is whether this train ran on a regular daily schedule over the BRT, or if it was a special departure hastily put together to compensate for service disruptions brought on by the strike. In either case, there was something wrong with the five-car train Luciano found at Kings Highway that evening.

The train was made up of typical BRT elevated equipment—five cars, each measuring 50 feet from end to end. Three of the cars were powered units—cars equipped with electric motors that provided propulsion power for the train. The other two were unpowered trailer cars that lacked electric motors of their own and were hauled along by the other three cars. A five-car train with three powered units and two trailers was common on BRT elevated lines in 1918. However, company operating rules specified that with such a train, the two nonpowered trailer cars could not be coupled together. At roughly

34,000 pounds, the trailers were much lighter than the powered cars (66,000 pounds), and better balance was achieved with an arrangement of powered car, trailer, powered car, trailer, powered car. Each of the five cars featured a steel underframe. However, the basic car body, including the roof, was constructed primarily of wood.

Luciano set himself up in the motorman's cab of the lead car, car 1064. This car was also equipped with trolley poles to draw electric current from the overhead wire along the surface-running portions of the Culver Line. The second car was another powered unit, car 725; it was followed by the two trailers, cars 100 and 80, coupled together. The third powered car, car 726, was on the rear. En route back to Brooklyn later in the evening, the train had reversed itself. The last car on the Manhattan-bound trip had become the lead car bound for Brooklyn; directly behind it were the two lightweight trailers, coupled together. This failure to observe proper procedure for arranging the train cars would contribute substantially to the death toll at the Malbone Street tunnel. Had the two trailer cars not been coupled together in violation of BRT rules, the Malbone Street Wreck might have been little more than an inconsequential derailment, a forgotten footnote in Brooklyn history. Table 4 displays additional information about the five cars.

Many questions can be asked in an effort to understand why the cars on Luciano's train were incorrectly coupled together. Unfortunately, this aspect of the Malbone Street Wreck was subjected to minimal analysis afterward, and little in the way of a documentary record was produced. The Brotherhood of Locomotive Engineers'

TABLE 4: The Five Cars of the Fatal Train

Car Number	Manufacturer	Year Built	Year Rebuilt
1064[a]	Stephenson	1903	—
725[b]	Pullman	1888	1905
100[c]	Gilbert	1887	1906
80[c]	Gilbert	1887	1906
726[b]	Pullman	1888	1905

[a] Built as an electric-powered car.

[b] Built as a trailer car for the Kings County Elevated Railroad for use behind steam engines; rebuilt by BRT into an electric-powered car.

[c] Built as a trailer car for Union Elevated Railroad for use behind steam engines; rebuilt by BRT into a trailer car for use between other electric-powered cars.

strike on November 1 involved motormen as well as motor-switch-men, the latter being responsible for coupling trains together in the yards. A degree of carelessness with respect to the proper makeup of trains on November 1 is certainly understandable if untrained indi-viduals coupled the fatal train together that day. All that is known is that two trailer cars were coupled together in violation of the BRT's operating rules.[4]

And so with an inexperienced and unqualified motorman in the cab, an improperly coupled five-car elevated train pulled out of Kings Highway yard on the BRT's Culver Line and headed for Park Row terminal in Manhattan. It was 5:15 P.M. The Malbone Street Wreck was now just 87 minutes away.

Luciano's train proceeded north along Gravesend Avenue (see ap-pendix B for a reconstructed schedule of the fatal train trip). Once he reached the Ninth Avenue station adjacent to Greenwood Ceme-tery—where today 15 victims of the Malbone Street Wreck are in-terred—the train altered its character. The trolley pole was pulled down and secured by rope to the gatework of car 1064, and the train began to draw its electric current from a track-side third rail. There was no more informal street running as on the old Culver Line. In-stead, the train headed up a ramp, curved onto the BRT's Fifth Ave-nue elevated line, and continued toward downtown Brooklyn. As he pulled out of the 36th Street station on the Fifth Avenue Line, Lu-ciano was but a block and a half from his home on 34th Street, where his wife and young daughter awaited his return from work.

More than likely, Luciano stopped at each station along the way to board and discharge passengers. However, because it was rush hour and passenger traffic was far heavier back to Brooklyn from Manhattan than in the opposite direction, it remains possible that the inbound trip carried no revenue passengers and Luciano by-passed station stops along the way.

To reach downtown Brooklyn, the BRT's Fifth Avenue elevated line curved from Fifth into Flatbush Avenue near the Long Island Railroad depot at Flatbush and Atlantic avenues. An earlier Long Island Railroad depot on this same site was the in-town terminal of the Brooklyn, Flatbush and Coney Island Railroad (1878 through 1882).[5] On November 1, 1918, construction crews were at work below ground adjacent to the depot, building "Section 2A of Route 12" of the Dual Subway System, the underground line that would soon allow Brighton Beach Line trains to eschew the old connection with the Fulton Street elevated train and travel to downtown Brooklyn and Manhattan by subway.

To gain access to the Brooklyn Bridge, the Fifth Avenue elevated connected with the Myrtle Avenue Line at Myrtle and Hudson avenues. Presently, Luciano reached the Sands Street station at the Brooklyn end of the bridge, the last stop before Manhattan, or—to borrow a later coinage—the "last exit for Brooklyn." Then it was over the famous bridge to the BRT's Manhattan terminal at Park Row, a short walk from City Hall. Just beyond City Hall was the old Post Office Building where, two months earlier, the War Labor Board had conducted hearings that were so instrumental in bringing on the BRT strike. Luciano's train from Kings Highway arrived at Park Row at 6:08 P.M.

With the opening of the Interborough subway's East River tunnel to Brooklyn a decade earlier, the inauguration of BRT elevated service across the Williamsburg Bridge in 1908, and the BRT's own Fourth Avenue subway reaching Manhattan in 1915 via the Manhattan Bridge, the press of passenger traffic at Park Row had eased off a bit and the Brooklyn Bridge was no longer the sole rapid transit gateway to Manhattan from Brooklyn. In pre-subway 1907, the BRT had dispatched 7,048 elevated cars across the Brooklyn Bridge every 24 hours, and crowded conditions at the Park Row terminal were frequently decried in angry newspaper accounts. By 1917, this number had fallen to 4,458, a reduction of 35 percent.

Despite lower patronage levels, Park Row was still a busy place in 1918; Luciano had no time to spare. BRT personnel were assigned to the terminal to assist incoming train crews with various tasks associated with turning a train around for its trip back to Brooklyn. The train was not, of course, literally turned around. Rather it was a case of Luciano disconnecting his motorman's control handles from one end of the five-car train, walking to the rear, and there establishing as the lead car the one that had been on the rear of the train. Metal plate line and destination signs had to be changed on all the cars, and signs reading "Culver Line" and "Park Row" were replaced with ones that read "Brighton Line" and "Brighton Beach." More than likely, Conductor Turner and his crew had taken care of this task as the train was headed over the Brooklyn Bridge to Manhattan minutes earlier.[6]

At the head of the train two matters required checking. A wooden sign reading "Brighton Beach Only"—black letters on a white background—had to be hung from the front platform of the lead car, and twin marker lights on the train's roof had to be set for the proper color code to indicate a Brighton Beach–bound train. (Marker lights were lantern-like devices that could display any of four colors—red, white, green, and yellow.) The sign checked out; it had probably been put in place back at Kings Highway. But on car 726, formerly the last car but now in the lead, the marker lights were not functioning and no color codes could be displayed.

From his days as a guard and a tower operator with the BRT, Luciano was surely aware of the need to display proper marker lights. While an inexperienced motorman trying to turn his train quickly at Park Row under some degree of pressure could easily have overlooked such a task, in this case no fault can be laid at Luciano's feet. The marker lights simply were not working. BRT rules anticipated such a possibility and stated that when marker lights could not be displayed, a single white lantern was to be hung from the front of the train. Luciano's train was so equipped. Investigators determined after the accident that a blown fuse was the reason the marker lights were inoperative.

After passengers had boarded the Brighton Beach–bound train, the crew members closed the gates at all four boarding locations. They relayed a two-bell signal from the rear end of the train up to the front that all was in readiness to proceed. Conductor Turner, now stationed between lead motor car number 726 and trailer car number 80, was the last link in the relay. When he reached up and pulled twice on the signal rope, he sounded a bell that was located just outside Luciano's cab on the opposite end of the car. The bell was more of a dull clank than a soft or sweet tone. Next to the motorman's cab and the bell was an advertisement that proclaimed "Horlick's, The Original Malted Milk" to anyone who looked up.

As a practical matter, a motorman could usually hear the progression of signal bells moving through the train from rear to front, even before the last and loudest signal sounded outside his cab. Upon hearing the final bell, Luciano let off the brakes by throwing a horizontally mounted handle over to one side with his left hand. This increased the air pressure in the train line and released the grip of brake shoes on each of the train's 40 steel wheels. The neophyte motorman then took hold of the controller with his right hand, pushed in the "deadman" button in the center of the handle, and swung the vertically mounted controller from its center-off position over to the right, all the while keeping pressure on the deadman button.[7] The train's lights flickered as current flowed to the motors. The five cars lurched forward. The train was off—off to Brooklyn and off to "Brighton Beach Only." Except it would never arrive there. It was 6:14 P.M. The Malbone Street Wreck was only 28 minutes away.

The train was crowded, but not excessively so. Luciano was aware of the need for caution while negotiating the Brooklyn Bridge, and he kept his train under control. On the upgrade out of Park Row he maintained full power; even so, the train labored and the speed was never more than 15 miles per hour. Nearing the crest of the bridge out over the dark, black waters of the East River, Luciano cut power; as the train started down into Brooklyn, he began to work the brake handle to keep his train under control for the descent to Sands Street. The speed limit for elevated trains crossing the Brooklyn Bridge was constant, upgrade or down—15 miles per hour.

From the center of the Brooklyn Bridge down into the Sands Street station, ironically enough, was an even steeper grade than the one from Crown Heights to Prospect Park that would soon prove to be Luciano's undoing.[8] That he was able to cross the Brooklyn Bridge safely suggests that his lack of experience with the particular configuration of the Brighton Beach Line was his more tragic shortcoming that November evening, not an inability to operate an elevated train on a steep, downhill grade.

Later, after the accident, surviving passengers faulted the quality of Luciano's overall skills at train operation; one of the first criticisms offered is that he overshot the station platform at Sands Street, the first station on the Brooklyn side of the bridge. Passenger Charles Darling, an attorney, described the start of the trip: "I was sitting in the front car of the train, directly behind the motorman's box. I realized as soon as we left Park Row that something was the matter. The car started and stopped with sharp jolts and jerks and it ran around the curve at Sands Street at a speed I considered dangerous."[9] Many other survivors voiced similar reactions.

Irregularly operated or not, Luciano's train left Sands Street and was routed onto the Fulton Street Line just south of there at Tillary Street. It rumbled along in front of Brooklyn's Borough Hall and picked up additional homeward-bound passengers at various stations in Brooklyn's business district—Boerum Place, Lawrence Street, and Elm and Duffield. Flatbush-bound passengers were headed home after a long day's work and were beginning to look beyond Saturday to the relaxation that Sunday would bring. Most, of course, were required to return to work on Saturday; in 1918 the luxury of a five-day work week was far from common, and at least a half day's work on Saturday was the norm. Luciano's five-car train continued out the Fulton Street Line toward the junction with the Brighton Beach Line at Franklin Avenue. At 6:29 P.M. the train pulled out of the station at Grand Avenue; Franklin Avenue was next, a quarter-mile away to the east.

At Franklin Avenue something happened that was accorded more attention after the accident than it deserved. Or perhaps better put, it was accorded attention for the wrong reasons.

Both the Fulton Street elevated and the Brighton Beach Line had their own separate station platforms at Franklin Avenue; the junction between the two lines was located to the west, or on the downtown side, of the station (see map 3). This junction was under the control of an operator stationed in a switch tower at the site, and approaching trains had to be routed onto their proper course just prior to entering the station. On duty in the Franklin Avenue tower that evening was a BRT employee named Peter Gorman; it was his task to determine where an approaching train was supposed to go and then align the switch tracks and set the semaphore signals to let it happen. The switch tracks and signals at a place like Franklin Avenue are known as an interlocking plant. The term refers to the way switches and signals are linked together mechanically so as to prevent a tower operator from routing one oncoming train into the path of another.

On an ordinary day, with trains following preestablished schedules, a towerman's tasks could be rather routine. This evening, though, schedules were in shambles because of the strike and Gorman had to be especially alert. No sooner had he dispatched a Brighton Beach–bound train around the curve from the Fulton Street Line onto the Brighton Beach Line than he looked up and saw another train following behind it. The approaching train had no marker lights displayed, and Gorman did not know where it was supposed to go. The "Brighton Beach Only" sign was unlit and offered him no help on a dark night and from a distance.

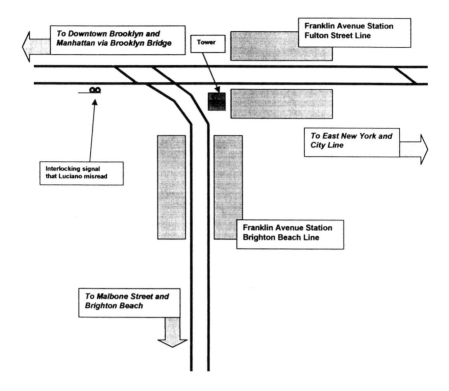

There were only two choices for a train coming from downtown Brooklyn: turn southward onto the Brighton Beach Line or continue eastward (straight ahead) out the Fulton Street elevated to City Line—the terminal of the Fulton Street Line at the Brooklyn-Queens border, so named because it was the city limits of Brooklyn prior to the 1898 municipal consolidation of Greater New York. Actually, some Fulton Street trains routinely terminated at Manhattan Junction in East New York, and not City Line. But that was not Gorman's problem at Franklin Avenue; he had only two choices for the approaching mystery train—straight ahead along Fulton Street or to the right and out the Brighton Beach Line.

Because the preceding train had been bound for Brighton Beach, Gorman made the reasonable guess that the train without marker lights was a Fulton Street train bound for City Line; he so set the switches and signals. "I guessed at it and gave him the top ball; guessed it for a City Line. We call it a ball; it is a signal; the top semaphore," said Gorman.[10]

An experienced motorman would have quickly realized that the combination semaphore and colored-light signals Gorman had displayed meant that the switch track was set for continuing out Fulton Street, not for turning southward onto the Brighton Beach Line. The proper course of action under such circumstances is to pull up short of the signal, stop the train, and sound four short blasts on the train's air whistle. This tells the tower operator that the signal is incorrect, something like a pitcher "shaking off" the catcher in baseball. But Luciano's lack of experience and motorman's skills tripped him up; either he failed to notice the signal, saw it and didn't understand what it meant, or saw it and understood what it meant but was unable to stop in a timely fashion. His train had passed the signal and entered the interlocking plant onto the incorrectly set switch before he stopped his train adjacent to the Franklin Avenue tower and shouted up to Gorman that his was a Brighton Beach–bound train. In fact, he had to climb out of his motorman's cab and walk out on the front platform of the lead car to talk with Gorman.

Luciano later claimed that he saw the signal at Franklin Avenue, knew what it meant, and assumed he was being sent out Fulton Street to City Line because of possible strike-related problems along the Brighton Beach Line. Even if this were true, BRT rules still called for stopping short of the incorrectly set signal and sounding four whistles.

What happened next was widely interpreted after the accident as further evidence of incompetence. However, it was anything but. Indecision and confusion may have caused Luciano to misidentify the signal Gorman had set and move his train through the incorrectly set switch. But to rectify the situation, Gorman and Luciano followed BRT procedures to a tee. Ironically, it was these procedures that passengers later thought were so hapless.

Although backing the train up a short distance to get clear of the switch track and then heading out the Brighton Beach Line as intended may have seemed like the simple and obvious correction of the mistake, backing up a train on a busy mainline railway is potentially dangerous and may only be done under carefully controlled conditions. Instead, Gorman had Luciano continue forward through the junction and beyond the Franklin Avenue station of the Fulton Street Line to a crossover between eastbound and westbound tracks that was located two blocks further west along the Fulton Street Line near Nostrand Avenue. Luciano then moved his motorman's station to the rear of the train and, after the crossover switches were properly

aligned, moved over the crossover to the westbound track and back
through the Franklin Avenue station to another crossover. Again he
changed ends, proceeded over this crossover, and this time was
routed correctly onto the Brighton Beach Line. The whole business
caused a delay of perhaps eight minutes. When Luciano finally
pulled into the Brighton Beach Line's station at Franklin Avenue it
was 6:38 P.M. The tragedy was now four minutes and 6,000 feet away.

Between Franklin Avenue and Prospect Park there were three stations—Dean Street, Park Place, and Consumers' Park. The first two
were required stops for all trains, and the third was a lesser station
where trains only stopped "on signal"; unless waiting passengers on
the platform set a signal to inform oncoming trains they wished to
board, or on-board passengers informed the conductor or a guard
they wished to get off, the motorman was not required to stop.

Luciano left Franklin Avenue at 6:38 P.M. and Dean Street at 6:39
P.M. At 6:40 P.M. the train crew forwarded their two-bell signals up
to the motorman's cab as they had at all previous stations. The train
was ready to leave Park Place for Prospect Park. It would never get
there. The Malbone Street Wreck was now less than two minutes
and 4,300 feet away.

But a linear distance of 4,300 feet is not all that separates the Park
Place station from the Malbone Street tunnel portal. There is also
the critical matter of height; Park Place is atop Crown Heights, and
the tunnel portal is at the foot of the hill. That drop is about 70
feet, and trains proceeding from Park Place to Malbone Street run
downhill almost the entire way.

Southbound trains are assisted in their acceleration out of Park
Place by virtue of the fact that the tracks immediately descend from
the elevated structure at this point and assume an alignment in a
below-grade, open cut. There is an ever-so-slight upgrade as the
right-of-way approaches a short, brick-lined tunnel under Eastern
Parkway that was built by the Brooklyn, Flatbush and Coney Island
Railroad in 1878. A hundred yards or so beyond Eastern Parkway the
steepest portion of the grade begins; it runs for 1,800 feet before
easing off again, but not entirely, as the right-of-way passes under a
bridge that carries Washington Avenue over the tracks at an oblique
angle just beyond the Consumers' Park station. It was while traveling
down this stretch of track between 6:41 and 6:42 P.M. that Luciano's

speeding train generated the momentum that became the physical force behind the Malbone Street Wreck.

Two factors combined to cause the crash. First, Luciano's general inexperience in rapid transit operation prevented him from realizing the importance of keeping his train under better control and making timely brake applications to retard speed on the downhill grade. But this was a man who within the hour had safely taken his train to Manhattan and back across the Brooklyn Bridge, which has a steeper grade than the hill down from Crown Heights.

Luciano's second and far more critical shortcoming was that he was unfamiliar with the route of the Brighton Beach Line and was unaware that a newly installed, sharp curve into a new tunnel awaited him at the foot of the draw. Before this new curve and tunnel had been placed in service several weeks earlier, southbound Brighton Beach Line trains continued directly ahead into the Prospect Park station on a course that was generally straight, although it included a modest curve immediately before the station platform. Luciano likely recalled this configuration and assumed it was still operational. A small sign at the side of the track immediately before the new curve posted the maximum speed motormen were allowed to maintain around the curve—six miles per hour. Thomas Blewitt's secretary, Edna Carroll, later testified that she clearly remembered typing up bulletin "L.S. 114" informing BRT personnel of the speed restriction at the time service was routed into the new tunnel in late September.

In 1918 the Brighton Beach Line lacked any system to monitor the speed of downhill trains and apply the brakes automatically if motormen exceeded the established limit. Such a system is practically universal on rapid transit lines today. The technology was available in 1918 and was being deployed throughout the network of new rapid transit lines being built under the terms of the Dual Subway Contracts. Neither the Fulton Street Line nor the segment of the Brighton Beach Line over Crown Heights, however, were so equipped in 1918. In later years, they would be.

Shortly after leaving the Park Place station at 6:40 P.M., Conductor Turner gave Luciano a three-bell signal. Such a communication, delivered while the train was under way, meant that the motorman must stop the train at the next station, whether scheduled to or not. As the next station was Consumers' Park, a flag stop, Turner was telling Luciano that he had passengers aboard the train who wished to get off. In addition, a small group of people had gathered on the southbound platform at Consumers' Park and had set the requisite signal there to inform the next train they wished to board.[11]

Luciano never stopped at Consumers' Park. Instead his train continued on the downhill grade through the station at a speed in excess of 30 miles per hour. It is unclear whether Luciano ever heard Turner's signal, or whether he heard it and had no idea what it meant, or whether he knew what it meant but was unable to do anything about it; all three are all possibilities. The same three options hold with respect to Luciano's reaction to the platform signal set by waiting passengers at the Consumers' Park station. As the front car of the train raced through Consumers' Park, the tunnel portal was only 900 feet down the track and the Malbone Street Wreck was a mere 15 seconds away.

Even this 15 seconds, though, could have been enough time for Luciano to throw his brakes into emergency and avoid the pending disaster. However, he failed to do so. Perhaps he was in a state of sheer panic in the cab and was unable to react to what was happening around him. Perhaps, on the other hand, he was unconcerned and believed that a routine brake application would eventually be adequate to stop the train at the next station, Prospect Park. His speed of approximately 30 miles per hour, while excessive for approaching a 6-mile-per-hour curve, was not in and of itself something to alarm a motorman who was ignorant of the lethal danger just ahead.

As the train raced through the Consumers' Park station with the Malbone Street tunnel a mere 900 feet down the track, Luciano had no way of seeing the tunnel portal. A slight curve in the right-of-way between Washington Avenue and Malbone Street masked the train's fate from its motorman. It was not until the first car was directly under Washington Avenue several critical seconds later that Luciano could possibly have first noticed that the rails his train was following did not continue straight ahead into the old Malbone Street tunnel but curved off sharply to the right. During these last few critical seconds, Luciano was unable to perceive—much less react to—this advanced warning, minimal as it might have. The night was dark, BRT elevated trains were equipped with no headlamps to illuminate the way, and the unskilled motorman lacked adequate knowledge of the Brighton Beach Line so as to appreciate the changes recently implemented at Malbone Street.

The train came out from under the Washington Avenue overpass. With less than 500 feet to impact, the possibility of the motorman's taking corrective action had just about run out. Most probably, Luciano never saw or knew what was in store until his speeding train began to heel into the curve itself.

Five months later at his trial for manslaughter, Luciano—who was carefully coached by BRT attorneys—gave a near-perfect recitation of the BRT book of rules and proposed it to be a factual description of his actions approaching the tunnel portal on November 1. He claimed that the regular brakes did not function. When he realized this, he said he applied the emergency brakes. He testified under oath that when the emergency brakes failed to bring the train under control, he threw the train into reverse and applied current to the motors—just as the company expected its properly trained motormen to do under such circumstances. But Edward Luciano did no such things. The regular brakes did not fail; the emergency brakes were never applied; reverse power on the electric motors was never called for. Documentary evidence obtained after the crash is clear on these points, as is seen in chapter 7.

Even if motorman Luciano never appreciated the need to apply the train's emergency brakes approaching the Malbone Street tunnel portal, four other men aboard the train should have sensed the danger and taken action themselves. Each of the four crew members was familiar with the Brighton Beach route, should have been aware of what was pending by virtue of the train's excessive speed, and knew that a novice was in the cab. Each had access to a safety valve that would have made the all-out emergency brake application Luciano never did. They failed to do so. In conductor Turner's case, this inaction was after and in full awareness of the fact that Luciano failed to make the Consumers' Park stop that Turner had ordered.

Immediately after the accident, Turner described the ride down from Crown Heights as a harrowing experience, unlike any in his years with the BRT. Later, after conversations with the BRT's legal staff, Turner's story changed. The ride became far less harrowing and he even denied giving the three-bell signal to stop at Consumers' Park.[12] Luciano's lack of experience in the motorman's cab is clearly the primary and immediate cause of the Malbone Street Wreck. But the failure of any of the train crew to seize control and apply the emergency brake is very difficult to explain.

At 6:42 P.M., car 726 started into the curve. The Malbone Street Wreck was happening. It would be over in a little more than 10 seconds. More than 650 people were aboard the five-car train; one out of every seven of them was about to be killed (see map 4).

The lead car, car 726, raced around the curve and entered the tunnel; it left the tracks. Although the front and rear corners of the car's roof hit against the tunnel wall, this car received relatively little damage. The real damage—and the bulk of the carnage—would take place in the two lightweight trailer cars, cars 80 and 100, which were coupled together directly behind the lead car. The jolt of the derailment of the lead car disrupted the rhythms of the trailer cars, and both of them derailed before they reached the concrete tunnel portal. Each came into contact with the outside face of the portal before being dragged into the tunnel by the continuing force of the train's forward momentum. In the case of car 80, its brush with the outside face of the tunnel portal was more of a glancing blow along its side after the forward portion of the car had entered the tunnel. Only the rear truck of the car derailed and its front truck stayed on the track. But car 100, the second trailer, hooked the face of the portal squarely with its left front corner. As it was then dragged forward into the tunnel, it was totally destroyed and would later be removed from the tunnel only as scrap and debris.

Once inside the tunnel, a more terrible fate awaited the two derailed trailer cars. They were no longer retained in the center of the tunnel by the guideway character of the rails. Instead, centrifugal force drove the two lightweight cars outward along and against the wall of the tunnel on the outside, or left side, of the entry curve. But the tunnel wall was not a flat or smooth surface; it was a structure whose vertical steel support columns extended out beyond the plane of the concrete wall itself, thus subjecting the cars to a horrible serration effect.

Car 100 was totally destroyed. Although the floor, underframe, right side, and end bulkheads of car 80 remained intact, its roof and left side were completely, almost surgically, cut away. Passengers seated on the side of these cars closest to the tunnel wall on the outside of the entry curve bore the heaviest casualties.

By the time the rearmost two cars in the five-car train—the other

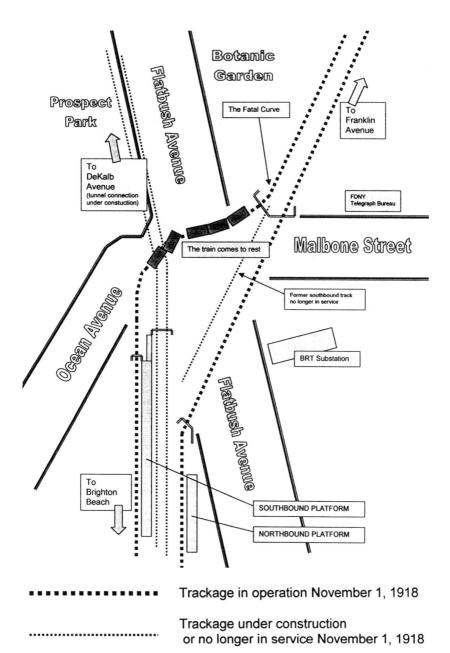

Prospect Park

Flatbush Avenue

Botanic Garden

The Fatal Curve

To Franklin Avenue

To DeKalb Avenue (tunnel connection under constuction)

FDNY Telegraph Bureau

The train comes to rest

Malbone Street

Former southbound track no longer in service

Ocean Avenue

BRT Substation

Flatbush Avenue

To Brighton Beach

SOUTHBOUND PLATFORM

NORTHBOUND PLATFORM

■■■■■■■■■■■■■■ Trackage in operation November 1, 1918

⋯⋯⋯⋯⋯⋯⋯ Trackage under construction
or no longer in service November 1, 1918

two powered cars, cars 725 and 1064—reached the curve into the tunnel portal, the train's speed was substantially reduced, even though mere seconds had passed since the accident had begun. These two cars stayed on the rails and, for all intents and purposes, the only damage they sustained was from flying debris from the second and third cars. The train came to rest inside the tunnel. The tail end of the rear car was 75 feet inside the tunnel. Luciano's lead car was approximately 145 feet shy of the end of the station platform at Prospect Park. One might say that he failed to reach safety by merely that much.

Had the two trailer cars not been coupled together in violation of BRT procedures, would the accident have been so severe? The lead car, car 726, obviously took the curve and entered the tunnel faster than any of the four following cars, yet this car was not badly damaged. It derailed and its roof made some contact with the tunnel wall, but its weight kept it in the general alignment of the tracks and it was not dragged along the tunnel wall as were the two lightweight trailer cars. The weak link in the train turned out to be the point where the two trailer cars were coupled together. This is the section of the train that deviated farthest from the alignment of the track before reaching the tunnel and then crashed violently into the portal of the tunnel. Neither trailer car was able to anchor the other; as a result, both were thrown mercilessly against the tunnel wall.[13]

By 6:42 P.M., the Malbone Street Wreck was over. Now the task became one of recovering the injured, removing the dead, adding up the toll, and finding out why the accident had happened. In the lead car, a dazed, frightened, and confused—but otherwise physically uninjured—Edward Luciano emerged from his motorman's cab. By the dim glow of some nearby light, Charles Darling frantically asked him what happened.

Much was said over the ensuing hours, days, weeks, months, and years in an effort to answer Darling's question. However, none of the reporting, testimony, conjecture, or analysis rivaled Luciano's first post-accident words as a truthful answer to Darling's question. "I don't know. I lost control of the damn thing. That's all."[14]

NOTES

1. Three racetracks were served by the Coney Island excursion railways. In June 1879, Brighton Beach Race Track opened adjacent to the Brighton

Beach Hotel; it was served by the Brooklyn, Flatbush and Coney Island Railroad. Sheepshead Bay Race Track, which opened in 1880, was located on the mainland side of Sheepshead Bay; it was served by the New York and Manhattan Beach as well as the Brooklyn, Flatbush and Coney Island and its successors. Finally, in 1886 the Brooklyn Jockey Club opened the Gravesend Race Track. It was located between Gravesend Avenue and Ocean Parkway to the south of Kings Highway and was served by the Prospect Park and Coney Island Railroad, as well as Long Island trains using Prospect Park and Coney Island tracks. Gravesend Race Track was also served by a branch line connecting to the New York and Sea Beach Railroad. By 1910, all three tracks were closed. For further information on thoroughbred horseracing in Coney Island, see Edo McCullough, *Good Old Coney Island* (New York: Fordham University Press, 1999), 114–53.

2. The Culver Line enjoyed an interesting history following its founding in 1875 as the Prospect Park and Coney Island Railroad. In 1893 the Prospect Park and Coney Island was purchased by the Long Island Railroad and was operated as an adjunct of the Long Island including through service over both systems via a connection at Gravesend Avenue just south of Foster Avenue. The BRT brought the Culver Line into its expanding system in 1898 by means of a lease that was not converted into a purchase until 1923. For further information on the transformation of the Prospect Park and Coney Island Railroad into an element of the BRT rapid transit system, see Karl F. Groh, "The South Brooklyn Railway," *Headlights* 55 (May-June 1993), 3–12.

3. I have only been able to determine the names of three of the four BRT personnel who worked aboard Luciano's train—Turner, Weinberg, and a man by the name of Samuel Rosoff. It is possible that one of the four positions was unfilled on November 1. In that event, the gates between two of the cars would have been unattended.

4. I have analyzed numerous photographs of BRT electric-powered elevated trains of this era taken on days other than November 1, 1918, and have found no other instances when unpowered trailer cars were coupled to each other. This hardly constitutes ironclad evidence, but it at least suggests that coupling unpowered trailer cars together was not common practice.

5. The new depot was opened in April 1907. At the same time, a subway was constructed under Atlantic Avenue for Long Island Railroad trains and they no longer had to operate at grade in the middle of the thoroughfare. See Vincent F. Seyfried, *The Long Island Railroad: A Comprehensive History* (Garden City, N.Y.: Author, 1961–1975), 7:24–42.

6. Metal plate signs were an earlier form of train identification that were later superceded by cloth signs mounted on rollers similar to window shades.

7. The deadman button was an important safety feature. If a motorman became incapacitated and released his hold on the button, the train's brakes were applied.

8. According to U.S. Geological Survey charts, the Brooklyn Bridge involves a 50-foot fall over a distance of 2,600 feet, while from Crown Heights to Malbone Street is a 70-foot fall over a distance of 4,300 feet.

9. *Brooklyn Eagle* (November 3, 1918), 3.

10. Memorandum, "In Re Wreck at the Malbone Street Cut of the Brighton Beach Line Tunnel; Facts Developed So Far," John F. Hylan Papers, box 197, folder 10, p. 5, Archives of the City of New York, New York.

11. The location of the Consumers' Park station has sometimes caused confusion. First of all, the station no longer exists. Second, a station near the top of the grade at Eastern Parkway, which is in operation today, did not exist in 1918. Although Consumers' Park is sometimes thought to have been the earlier name of the Eastern Parkway station, this is incorrect. Consumers' Park station was 850 feet north of Malbone Street near the intersection of Washington Avenue and Montgomery Street.

12. See "Guard Never Had So Wild Ride as That Preceding Accident," *Brooklyn Times* (November 2, 1918), 3. For Turner's views five months later during Luciano's manslaughter trial, see *Brooklyn Times* (April 3, 1919), 1.

13. Guard Morris Weinberg, whose position was between the second and third cars, was the only crew member killed in the accident. He was likely riding immediately inside either the second or third car close to the point where they were coupled together.

14. *Brooklyn Eagle* (November 1, 1918), 1.

CHAPTER 6

The Rescue

Although the first fire alarm calling rescue forces to the site of the Malbone Street Wreck was rung into the fire department's headquarters on Jay Street in downtown Brooklyn at 6:44 P.M., two minutes after the accident, it was almost half-past seven before reasonable numbers of properly equipped personnel were on the scene and at work.[1] The disaster took place in the very middle of one of the busier intersections in all of Brooklyn—the spot near the Willink Entrance to Prospect Park where Malbone Street, Ocean Avenue, and Flatbush Avenue all intersect—but the wrecked train and its passengers were wedged in a narrow tunnel under the intersection and were not in a readily accessible location. Responding companies from the New York Fire Department who performed the bulk of the rescue work that evening were faced with a disaster that was as much a cave-in as a train wreck. This was particularly true in the second of the two trailer cars that comprised the train, car 100. The 50-foot car was so mangled in the crash that, when the train came to rest, the car's wreckage had been compressed into a space that was a little more than 40 feet from one end to the other.

The first task rescue forces faced was simply gaining access to track level. Whether inside the tunnel or outside of it in the open cut, this was a good 15 or more feet below street level. Three principal corridors of access and egress between the railway right-of-way and street level were established. The more direct was up and down as many ladders as the fire department could set up between the area near the tunnel portal and Malbone Street at a point just to the east of Flatbush Avenue. The second was out through the front of the lead car of the train, down the tunnel to the Prospect Park station, along the southbound platform of the new station, and then up to street level at Lincoln Road and what was then the station's only functioning entrance. The distance between the station entrance on Lincoln Road and the Malbone Street tunnel portal where the ladders were set up was a little more than 1,000 feet. Still another helpful path that rescue personnel used was between the Lincoln Road entrance and the Malbone Street tunnel portal along the northbound track of the Brighton Beach Line. Needless to say, rapid transit service was suspended in both directions.

Medical personnel were dispatched to the scene to tend to those who had been injured. Getting the more seriously injured away from the site to proper hospital facilities became the next task. Although conventional ambulances were sent from all over Brooklyn to assist, work by an organization called the Women's Volunteer Corps, using largely private automobiles, was invaluable in allowing the evacuation to take place in a timely fashion. As many as 200 injured passengers were transported to local hospitals that evening. It was reported that women victims were sometimes difficult to identify because many had become separated from their handbags; men, on the other hand, tended to carry on their persons a new form of documentation that facilitated identification—draft cards.

The very first people in Brooklyn to know that a disaster had taken place at Malbone Street—aside from those unfortunate souls who were aboard Luciano's train—were in all probability passengers on the platform at Consumers' Park who wished to board the Brighton Beach–bound train but were unable to when Luciano failed to stop at the station. Because of the way the track curves slightly after passing Consumers' Park station and then curves again even more sharply into the tunnel, there was not a direct line of sight between the southbound platform there and the tunnel portal. But the passengers waiting on the platform knew disaster had struck when they heard the sound of the crash and saw a brilliant display of blue pyrotechnics as the derailed train tore the ground-level third rail loose from its moorings and electrical discharges lit up the dark night sky.

Many of the passengers at Consumers' Park station set off on foot along the railroad right-of-way to investigate. They became the first outsiders to reach the scene, but there was little they could do. It was dark at the portal; inside the tunnel, where the train had plunged minutes before, it was even darker. Screams and other indescribable sounds of human agony could be heard from within. Shortly, passengers from the last car, physically less seriously injured but in varying states of shock, began to wander and stumble out of the tunnel. Those who had walked to the site from Consumers' Park at first just stood aside and stared in disbelief at these first emerging survivors of the Malbone Street Wreck. Presently they regained their wits and offered whatever comfort they could, pending the arrival of trained rescue personnel. Among them was a detective in the New York City Police Department named John McCarthy, who gathered scraps of wood and started a bonfire to provide some minimal illumination and warmth.

Up beyond the lead car of the train a different tableau unfolded. A young newsboy named Willie Connell, who lived on the other side of the park at 168 Prospect Park Southwest, waited each night on the platform of the Prospect Park station for the arrival of bundles of late editions that were regularly transported on the open front and rear platforms of specified BRT elevated trains. Many New York newspapers were printed near the BRT's Park Row terminal in Manhattan, and the printing plant of Brooklyn's own *Daily Eagle* was just a stone's throw from the Sands Street elevated complex near Borough Hall. Use of elevated trains for newspaper delivery, especially for time-sensitive late editions that were delivered during the middle of the evening rush hour, was sensible and efficient.

On November 1, 1918, young Connell, together with his dog, was waiting for evening newspapers at the Prospect Park station when Luciano's train came to grief in the tunnel just before the station. The youngster had no idea what was happening in the tunnel—the sounds were like nothing he had ever heard before. Soon he saw a man walk out of the tunnel in the middle of the tracks in a complete daze. In all likelihood this was Edward Luciano, the motorman, who left the scene almost immediately and made his way home. When arrested by police later in the evening, Luciano had no recollection of how he had gotten home but thought he might have taken a streetcar. (A plausible route would have been the BRT's Church Avenue Line, which operated across Flatbush a mile or so beyond the scene of the accident; it would have left him off at Fourth Avenue and 39th Street, five blocks away from his home on 34th Street between Third and Fourth avenues.)

The circumstances surrounding Luciano's arrest were unusual. Home was his initial and perhaps even instinctive destination, and he probably got there between eight and nine o'clock. Shortly afterward, he either went by himself or was taken by BRT officials to company offices located in the nearby 36th Street yards. Detectives from the New York City Police Department were sent to find Luciano; when they reached his home, his wife Josephine told them that he was not there and she did not know where he was. Suspicious, one of the detectives then placed a telephone call to BRT headquarters; claiming to be a local druggist who had been instructed to deliver a prescription to Luciano, he was told the motorman was at 36th Street. That is where the detectives found him and took him into custody. They escorted him to the police station on Snyder Avenue in Flatbush where the investigation was being coordinated. When queried by reporters as he was led into the Snyder Avenue facility, Edward Luciano said; "A man has to make a living."[2] After several hours of interrogation, Luciano was arraigned before a magistrate in Flatbush Court and ordered held without bail.

Meanwhile, back at Malbone Street, the rescue effort continued. It is neither necessary nor helpful to retell stories of horror and gore associated with the accident, except to note that there was more than enough of it. It was during the initial hours after the crash that a good deal of misinformation about the Malbone Street Wreck was generated, some of which has never been corrected and continues to be repeated in occasional Sunday supplement stories about the disaster. It has been claimed, for instance, that many people who survived the crash itself were later electrocuted when BRT workers in the electric power department ill-advisedly restored current to the damaged third rail. This is not true.[3]

Standard procedure on most electric railways, at least until the advent of two-way radio communication in a later era, was that if circuit breakers "blew" at a substation or powerhouse cutting off electricity, current was quickly restored. If they blew a second time, current stayed off until officials could investigate the situation. Circuit breakers in the BRT's electrical substation on Flatbush Avenue adjacent to the Prospect Park station first cut out at 6:42 P.M. when the southbound third rail was torn away by the careening train entering the Malbone Street tunnel. (This, in fact, was how the time of the accident was firmly established.) The breakers were reset within a minute or so, but when power surged through the damaged circuits the breakers immediately cut out again; this time they stayed off. This all happened long before any large number of survivors could possibly have taken to the roadbed to seek safety, making the stories of their electrocution while emerging from the tunnel most unlikely. But even if this is conjecture, there is also documentary evidence to discount the electrocution stories. None of the 93 death certificates issued for fatal victims of the Malbone Street Wreck cite electrocution as a principal or contributory cause of death.

Additional examination of these same 93 certificates allows certain conclusions of a forensic nature to be drawn. The overwhelming majority of deaths in the Malbone Street Wreck—88 of the 93, or 95 percent—were caused by massive skull injuries. Of these 93 death certificates, 76 show the Malbone Street tunnel as the place of death. Only eight victims survived beyond November 1 to die on following days.[4] Thus, for most people who were killed in the tragedy, death was probably swift.

It is safe to assume that, because trailer cars 100 and 80 were so totally mangled when they came into contact with the tunnel wall, a disproportionate number of passengers who were seated on long, lengthwise benches on the left sides of these two cars were fatally injured in the crash. Passengers in the second and third cars who survived the accident were probably those who were seated on the right side of the train.

The shock and the fear that the accident triggered throughout Brooklyn made the night of November 1 and the early morning hours of November 2 a time of horror in the borough. As word of the tragedy spread through the residential precincts of Flatbush and its environs, where the majority of Brighton Beach Line passengers lived, fear was compounded by the fact that the accident completely shut down regular rapid transit service from downtown Brooklyn and Manhattan over the Brighton Beach Line. Many homeward-bound people who were perfectly safe were either stranded aboard subsequent trains stalled back along the line or rerouted over some alternative and longer course, thus delaying arrival home and reassurances to loved ones there. BRT streetcar service along Flatbush Avenue, Malbone Street, and Ocean Avenue past the site of the crash was necessarily suspended, further complicating travel and communication between downtown Brooklyn and Flatbush. Brooklyn's telephone network, already operating under severe limitations because of personnel shortages brought on by the influenza epidemic, quickly reached a state of complete overload. Families waited; accounts of the Malbone Street Wreck spread, often with grotesque distortions of fact—even though the truth itself was quite horrible enough.

The overall rescue effort was less an exercise in heroism than it was plain hard work under difficult and gruesome conditions. Stores along Flatbush Avenue near the site were used as temporary aid stations—and temporary morgues, as well. As many as 50 less seriously injured passengers were treated in a temporary aid station set up in nearby Ebbets Field. When Charles Ebbets Jr. heard about the accident, his first thought was that his father, Charles Ebbets Sr.—the man who had built Ebbets Field—might have been aboard the fatal train. When he learned that his father was not, he placed the ball park at the disposal of authorities for rescue-related purposes.

Many later spoke in admiration of the efforts put forth by two unidentified sailors—passengers aboard the train—during the rescue effort. "They seemed to have superhuman strength," one rescue worker said. "They worked for hours steadily, and then went away without telling who they were."[5] Ironically, of three fatally injured passengers aboard the train who were not local residents, one was a member of the U.S. Navy, assigned to the Naval Shipyard in Brooklyn (see appendix C). One can only wonder if the two sailors whose rescue work was so applauded were traveling with the sailor who was fatally injured.

Lack of adequate lighting in and around the tunnel was a liability as rescue work began. Fire and police forces arrived with lanterns, but quickly went door-to-door in the vicinity seeking more of them from local residents. Bonfires were continued near the portal, using lumber that was at hand from the still incomplete construction project at the site; this gave rise to some false accounts in the next day's press that the fatal train had itself caught fire. Eventually both the Brooklyn Gas Company and the Brooklyn Edison Company supplied portable lighting units to the site, including lights strung through the tunnel itself.

Several clergymen came to the scene of the accident Friday evening to care for the victims; they did not restrict their ministrations to spiritual matters. As needed, they lent a hand with more secular aspects of the rescue effort. One of four Roman Catholic priests who was on the scene was a young man who would later enjoy a distinguished career in Brooklyn education. The Reverend William J. Dillon served as president of St. Joseph's College in Brooklyn in the years after the Second World War. On November 1, 1918, he was a newly ordained curate assigned to St. Francis of Assisi parish on Nostrand Avenue near Malbone Street, a little over a half mile from the site of the crash.[6]

Medical and rescue workers were not the only people who put in long hours on the night of November 1, 1918. Political operatives toiling on behalf of contending candidates in the gubernatorial election that was only four days away were also kept busy on into the evening. A full-page advertisement ran in the *Brooklyn Eagle* on November 2—less than 24 hours after the tragedy—calling on Brooklyn voters to "turn out" the man (the incumbent governor) who had appointed the current membership of the state's Public Service Commission (PSC). The ad was signed "Citizens Committee for Alfred E. Smith," and the reference to the PSC, which exercised regulatory control over many aspects of the BRT, was a crude attempt to link Governor Whitman with the tragic events of the previous night.[7] Smith quickly repudiated the ad.

The Malbone Street Wreck put severe pressure on Brooklyn's hospital facilities, which were already under enormous strain because of the Spanish influenza epidemic. Hundreds of victims were transported to at least a half-dozen different facilities. The greatest volume was sent to Brooklyn's principal medical facility, Kings County Hospital. The campus-like grounds of the hospital were less than a mile from the site of the crash, and it was here that the Kings County morgue was located. It was to the morgue that bodies were taken for final examination and the issuance of requisite death certificates. Of the 93 fatal casualties of the Malbone Street Wreck, 81 death certificates were issued at the Kings County morgue; the other 12 were issued in other borough hospitals. It was also to the Kings County morgue that fearful and grieving loved ones came all through the night and on into the next day to identify the dead.

By late Friday night, the police department had compiled the first lists of casualties at its Snyder Avenue police station, headquarters for the overall rescue effort. Many panic-stricken people first sought information there; personal effects of wreck victims were also collected there. The *Brooklyn Eagle* attempted to post similar lists at its local office on Flatbush Avenue near Linden Boulevard, but the accuracy of all these early tabulations was very imperfect. Injured passengers who would fully recover were listed among the dead; misspelling of names caused further uncertainties. Thus, people had to go to the Kings County morgue for definitive information about missing loved ones, where it was not until the early hours of Saturday morning that morgue physicians completed their tasks and bodies were available for identification. So active was the traffic at the morgue and so many were the victims, that an initial decorum of covering bodies with white shrouds except while they were being examined or identified had to be abandoned. The size of the morgue building itself quickly proved inadequate, so a laundry building adjacent to it that was still under construction was pressed into service as an additional place where people could identify victims.[8]

The scene at Kings County Hospital in the hours after the Malbone Street Wreck may well have been the most ghastly public experience ever to befall Brooklyn. More than a dozen police officers were assigned to control and supervise crowds at the morgue, and one of them put it this way to reporters: "There is no place else on earth that I would not rather be than here."[9]

In a tableau that was repeated in one fashion or another throughout Flatbush that weekend, on Saturday morning a woman met her cousin on the street as they were both headed for church. (November 2 is a special day of prayer for Roman Catholics—ironically enough, prayers for the deceased.) The latter had not heard of the previous night's tragedy but, as they spoke, they realized that a third cousin—a young Irish immigrant named Michael Gilbert who rented a room in the second woman's house—usually traveled home from work each evening aboard the Brighton Beach Line. They rushed to the house and opened the door to young Gilbert's room. The bed had not been slept in, and there was no sign of him. Later in the day they identified his body in the morgue at Kings County Hospital. Gilbert had been riding home on November 1 with yet another cousin, Michael Ryan, also a recent Irish immigrant. Ryan, too, was among the 93 fatalities of the Malbone Street Wreck, and the two men are one of four sets of family members who perished together in the disaster—one husband and wife; two sisters; Gilbert and Ryan; and the only trio, two brothers and their cousin (see appendix C).

Once passengers, living and dead, had been evacuated from the wreck, the next task was to remove the train from the tunnel. On the evening of November 1, a wrecker train was dispatched west along the Fulton Street elevated line from the BRT's yards in East New York, but it was never able to reach Malbone Street. For one thing, electricity had been shut off in the third rail between Franklin

Avenue and Prospect Park. For another, the police department had
impounded the fatal train at the crash site and would not allow people associated with the transit company to get near it. Under the
direction of Kings County District Attorney Harry Lewis, photographs were to be taken and evidence gathered for possible criminal
prosecution. In addition, BRT personnel were to be prevented from
doing anything to the train that might compromise the state's case.
(Lewis, the district attorney, was no kin to the motorman sometimes
called Lewis but whose real surname was Luciano.)

The effort to preserve evidence was futile. Neither the police nor
District Attorney Lewis and his staff had any idea what to look for
aboard the train to determine what happened in the minutes and
seconds before the crash. The train itself was a treasure trove of clues
as to what Luciano did—and, more important, what he failed to do.
But it was BRT officials, once they were given access to the train,
who discovered these clues.

It was not until Sunday afternoon, November 3, that company
personnel were allowed back into the tunnel to take control of the
train. A team of experts led by the BRT's superintendent of equipment, William G. Gove, supervised the rerailing of the cars that were
off the tracks. The team conducted preliminary tests of the train's
braking apparatus at the scene, and they observed and documented
the condition of all five cars. The BRT team was accompanied by an
engineer from the PSC, as well as by experts from the Westinghouse
Traction Brake Company. Car 100, of course, was not rerailed; it was
removed from the tunnel in the form of debris. Its trucks, however,
were taken back to the BRT's 36th Street shops for further analysis,
and the car's all-important triple valve—the device that responds to
air pressure changes in the train line and controls the application of
a car's brakes—was also removed and returned to 36th Street after
being carefully marked and identified in the presence of witnesses at
the scene.

Once BRT crews had rerailed the train, they hauled it back to
36th Street. The four-car train followed a route that largely retraced
Luciano's ill-fated course of 48 hours earlier. It was hauled back over
Crown Heights to Fulton Street, then along the Fulton Street line
to Sands Street, and back to 36th Street from Sands Street via the
Myrtle Avenue and Fifth Avenue lines. The trip did not go smoothly.
While passing through the so-called Bridge Yard near Sands Street

station in downtown Brooklyn, the train derailed. It was an operational inconvenience, though, not another tragedy. BRT elevated service across the Brooklyn Bridge had to be suspended for several hours
until the mishap was cleared up and the trip to 36th Street resumed.

After all investigations were completed, the BRT decided that car
80 was too badly damaged to warrant rebuilding; it was scrapped,
just as car 100 had been. The other three cars were repaired and
restored, and they remained in service on Brooklyn elevated lines
until after the Second World War.

The horror of November 1, 1918, was still fresh in everyone's mind
when a dispute erupted between the BRT and the PSC. Under provi-
sions of the Dual Subway Contracts that the PSC was monitoring
and managing, the city of New York and the BRT had entered a
financial relationship that called for each party to invest capital for
the construction of new transit routes. A similar contract was in effect between the city and the Interborough Rapid Transit Company.

The bonds that both the municipal government and the private
transit company would sell to raise this money were to be serviced
by income the BRT realized from fares passengers paid to ride the
company's subway and elevated lines. Before allocating such income
to bond service, though, the BRT was entitled to pay its actual operating expenses—the day-to-day costs of running the railway.

On November 14, 1918, the BRT wrote to the PSC advising the
state agency that it planned to regard all expenses associated with
the Malbone Street Wreck, including costs arising from anticipated
civil actions, as operating expenses. This touched a raw nerve at the
PSC. The traction company was saying, in so many words, that it
would pay off Malbone Street claims before it set aside money to
share with the city for Dual Subway Contracts debt service.

The PSC shot back a prompt reply saying this would not be permitted. The BRT then declared that it and the PSC were in formal
disagreement over a specific interpretation of the Dual Subway Contracts and requested that the matter be submitted to binding arbitration as was provided for under the terms of the contracts
themselves. Each party would nominate its own arbitrator, and these
two would then select a neutral third party to complete the team.[10]

This arbitration process was proceeding when in December 1918
a different kind of legal action was initiated that added an entirely

new dimension to the matter of civil claims associated with the Malbone Street Wreck. This development is discussed in chapter 7.

NOTES

1. While the New York Fire Department's (FDNY's) Brooklyn dispatching office was located in its Jay Street headquarters in downtown Brooklyn, a brand new neoclassical building had been completed in 1914 at 35 Malbone Street, immediately adjacent to the site of the accident. It became FDNY's Brooklyn dispatching center in 1923 and has so served ever since. FDNY units that responded to the Malbone Street Wreck included Engine Companies 219, 249, and 280, and Hook and Ladder Companies 113 and 132. Interestingly enough, if a first alarm response were to be sent today to FDNY's Brooklyn box 1082—adjacent to the site of the Malbone Street Wreck—the same five companies would be dispatched—plus Engine Company 248. Engine companies 219 and 280, and Hook and Ladder companies 113 and 132 occupy the very same fire houses today that they did in 1918.

2. *New York Times* (November 2, 1918), 1.

3. See, for example, John W. Newton, "The Malbone Street Crash," *New York Daily News Magazine* (November 6, 1988): 14–5.

4. Kings County death certificates for the year 1918 may be found in the Archives of the City of New York, 31 Chambers Street, Manhattan. I have concluded that 93 individuals were killed in the mishap by cross-checking names listed in the press as either killed or injured with an alphabetical index to the death certificate file, plus reviewing all death certificates issued in Kings County during the month of November 1918. There is no definitive, or official, casualty toll. Weeks and months after the accident, different newspapers continued to cite different numbers. Many months later in mid-1919, for example, the *New York Times* and *New York Herald* spoke of 92 fatal injuries in the Malbone Street Wreck, while the *Brooklyn Eagle* reported 97. I have identified and confirmed 93 fatal casualties (see appendix C). It remains entirely possible, however, that the actual toll is somewhat higher. Any such victims might have been hospitalized on November 1 and either not listed as injured or else grossly misidentified; upon expiring over the next several days, they may have had pneumonia cited as the cause of death, with no reference to the Malbone Street Wreck noted on the death certificate.

5. *Brooklyn Times* (November 2, 1918), 1.

6. Other clergy on the scene included Monsignor John T. Woods and the Reverend Francis Coppinger from Holy Cross parish on Church Avenue, and the Reverend Francis X. Ludeke from St. Francis. Dillon's friend

and colleague Monsignor Francis FitzGibbon noted in a recent letter to me that Dillon "did not speak of [the Malbone Street Wreck] often but when he did he said it was the most horrifying experience he ever had." FitzGibbon, who was a student at Brooklyn Prep in 1918, also writes: "I returned to class on Monday and walked over to see the site. It was in a railroad cut and you could view it from above."

7. *Brooklyn Eagle* (November 2, 1918), 8.

8. The morgue of 1918 no longer stands; on the site is a multistory neurology building. Attached to the rear of this structure, though, is a small two-story wing that hospital plot plans suggest could be a remnant of the old morgue. The laundry building still stands, although it no longer serves that function. All these structures are on the Winthrop Street side of the hospital grounds near Kingston Avenue.

9. *Brooklyn Times* (November 2, 1918), 2.

10. Public Service Commission for the First District, *Report for the Year Ending December 31, 1918* (Albany, N.Y.: J. B. Lyon Company, 1919), 1:146–8.

CHAPTER 7

The Investigation and Trials

With respect to the Malbone Street Wreck, the wheels of justice began to turn very quickly. How well or how effectively they turned, however, is an entirely different matter.

It took an ex-judge sitting in City Hall as mayor to know of a little-used provision in the city charter that permitted him to designate himself a "committing magistrate" and call witnesses, take testimony, and begin the task of establishing blame for the tragedy. Thus, on November 2, 1918—less than 24 hours after the accident—a formal proceeding got under way in Flatbush Magistrate's Court on Snyder Avenue, a facility that was located in the very same building where the rescue effort was still being coordinated.[1]

The presiding magistrate was John Francis Hylan, mayor of the city of New York. Hylan had been elected to the first of two four-year terms as mayor in November 1917. Although born and raised in Ulster County in upstate New York, his political base was Brooklyn; he was affiliated with the Brooklyn branch of the Democratic party rather than the Manhattan Democratic organization known as Tammany Hall. Among the many causes His Honor championed with unquenchable zeal was the proposition that private corporations had no business earning profits operating public mass transit services. Such responsibilities would be far better executed by the public sector, Hylan firmly believed, clear of all the distractions of profit, loss, stocks, bonds, and corporate interest.

Although Hylan had as little use for the Interborough Rapid Transit Company as he did for the Brooklyn Rapid Transit Company (the BRT) and sought to drive both from the municipal scene, he had a special antipathy for the Brooklyn-based company. Some have traced Hylan's feelings to the fact that as a young man he had been fired by a predecessor company of the BRT. Hylan himself did not hesitate to talk about the episode; in fact he said he bore the company no ill will since it caused him to take stock of his life and turn to a career in the law.[2] But he still believed the private sector and public mass transit were incompatible.

Hylan, who passionately championed causes in which he believed, did not enjoy his finest hours in reacting to the Malbone Street Wreck. So totally was he engulfed by a desire to embarrass higher officials of the BRT in the days and weeks after the accident, that his actions assumed a comic dimension and severely distorted the orderly quest for justice.

Hylan's first session on Saturday, November 2, was quite brief. After midnight in the presence of reporters mere hours after the accident and with emotions running high, the mayor promised that he would institute formal proceedings later that very same day. But he and his people quickly realized that serious preparation was required in the way of identifying witnesses and developing lines of questioning before a useful inquiry could be held. Thus, the Saturday session was adjourned less than five minutes after it began, the nominal reason cited being the inadequate size of the Snyder Avenue courtroom. The hearings reconvened in downtown Brooklyn on Monday, November 4, in the old County Court House at 145 Schermerhorn Street, a larger facility and one located much closer to such Kings County resources as the district attorney's office on Court Street.

Once under way, Hylan's proceedings bore less similarity to anything judicial than to a phenomenon associated in our own day with a different branch of government, a congressional investigation. Proper criminal trials would take place later and would stem from indictments handed down by a grand jury. Hylan the politician, on the other hand, was hardly concerned with technicalities such as rules of evidence, and he approached his task as anything but an open-minded jurist. Convinced in his bones that BRT management was criminally at fault in the disaster, he was determined to build a public record that documented his conviction.

Hylan was also involved in a bitter and continuing feud with the three commissioners of the Public Service Commission for the First District (the PSC) on all kinds of public transportation matters. Appointed by the state's Republican governor and responsible for implementing the Dual Subway Contracts that Hylan believed were a mistake from the outset, the PSC was a perfect target for Hylan's fury. In what can only be called tasteless opportunism, he used the hearings to suggest that the stewardship of the PSC was so flawed that it, too, must be cited as contributory to the accident and all the death and suffering it brought about. These Hylan-PSC contretemps shared front-page space in New York newspapers the day after the Malbone Street Wreck, as the mayor lashed out at the state agency and claimed that it was somehow responsible for the terrible tragedy of the previous evening.[3]

The Hylan hearings were as emotional as they were ideological. Survivors presented consistently critical accounts of Luciano's herky-jerky manner of train operation, and nothing was spared in describing the horror in the Malbone Street tunnel that evening. Because there was no cross-examination built into the process, there was little challenge offered to participants' statements, including occasional emotional outbursts from members of the audience. BRT workers, supervisors, and executives testified in a forthcoming manner, although some executives tried unsuccessfully to link their participation with a grant of immunity from any subsequent prosecution.

An ad hoc citizens organization emerged during Hylan's hearings. Called the Brighton Beach Survivors and Passengers Protective Association, the group represented individuals who had been injured aboard the fatal train as well as family members of people who were killed. Understandably, the group had very little good to say about the BRT, its management, or the general level of safety on the Brighton Beach Line. Their views were quite consistent with the direction Hylan was taking in his hearings. There was speculation in the press that some of the more emotional outbursts during the Hylan hearings were instigated by the BRT to help lay the groundwork for a change of venue during any subsequent legal proceedings.[4]

Between November 4, when Hylan held the first extended hearing in downtown Brooklyn, and December 11, when he announced that the inquiry was closed, approximately a half-dozen separate public sessions were conducted; all received extensive press coverage. In the end, Hylan, in his role of magistrate, concluded that the crime of manslaughter had been committed, and he directed that six individuals be charged.[5]

These same six men would soon be indicted for felony manslaughter by a Kings County grand jury, but it was despite—and not because of—Hylan's undisciplined and almost carnival-like proceedings. In a completely separate legal process that was carefully managed by District Attorney Harry Lewis, the November term of the Kings County grand jury handed down a series of criminal indictments against the same six individuals on December 19, 1918.[6]

BRT attorneys immediately petitioned the court for a change of venue. The BRT had conducted a postal-card poll of its transit passengers in an effort to develop statistical evidence demonstrating that the Hylan hearings had so prejudiced potential Kings County jurors that a fair trial in Brooklyn would be completely impossible.[7] However, many outraged citizens did not respond to the survey as requested but instead mailed the card to Mayor Hylan to bolster his case against the BRT.[8]

The BRT's petition for a change of venue was not a difficult one to argue, particularly given the amount of anti-BRT rhetoric that had been put on the public record during the hearings held by Mayor Hylan. Kings County Justice Almet F. Jenks, of the Appellate Division of the New York State Supreme Court, issued a show-cause order on January 3, 1919, requiring the state to demonstrate why a change of venue should not be granted. District Attorney Lewis and his staff were unequal to the task, and on January 28 Justice Callaghan issued a change of venue and ordered the trials moved from Kings County to Mineola in Nassau County.[9]

Motorman Luciano and five other individuals were indicted for manslaughter. One was Thomas F. Blewitt, the superintendent of the BRT's southern division—and the man who, on November 1, pronounced that Luciano was a qualified motorman. The other four held higher ranks in the BRT and its various associated companies. They included Timothy S. Williams, the company's president; vice president John Dempsey, who also bore the title of superintendent of transportation; William S. Menden, the line's chief engineer; and John H. Hallock, president of New York Consolidated Railroad, the BRT subsidiary that technically was the operator of Brighton Beach Line trains.

The prosecution sought and obtained Menden's indictment because he was responsible for engineering and construction on the BRT, and they spent a good deal of time inquiring as to whether the curve into the Malbone Street tunnel might have been a factor in the accident because of improper design, poor construction, or both.

Each defendant was indicted on four counts; each count was for the wrongful death of but one individual. Two Malbone Street victims, Edward Erskine Porter and Thomas Gilfeather, were selected to "represent" the other 91; among the victims, these two men were closest to acquiring celebrity status. In the death of Porter, each of the six defendants was indicted twice, once for first- and once for second-degree manslaughter; in the death of Gilfeather, each of the six was twice indicted in the same manner.[10]

The BRT provided and paid for a full battery of attorneys to represent the defendants, including Luciano. It was clearly in the railway's interest to provide the motorman with top-notch counsel, since to do otherwise might jeopardize the cases against the others. Use of company-provided counsel also precluded Luciano's reliance on any defense strategies that would have sought to lay blame for the accident on other BRT personnel or on the company itself.

After the change of venue was granted, the BRT took pains to ensure that its Brooklyn-based lawyers were properly and cordially received in the possibly alien world of Nassau County jurisprudence. The company retained two Long Island judges as part of the legal team and one of them, Judge Lewis J. Smith, put on an especially spirited summation in the Luciano trial. The BRT's recruitment of members of the judiciary on its defense team drew criticism from many quarters and soon resulted in state legislation outlawing such practices.

Over a 13-month period beginning in March 1919, five separate trials were held in Mineola—each of one individual; the prosecution failed to obtain a single conviction. Luciano, Blewitt, Dempsey, and Menden were all acquitted. The fifth trial was an earlier prosecution of Dempsey that ended in a hung jury. Finally, on January 17, 1921, District Attorney Lewis moved for the dismissal of all remaining indictments before Justice Edward Lazansky; the motion was granted and thus ended the state's effort to find criminal fault in the Malbone Street Wreck. The indictments against Timothy Williams and John Hallock were never brought to trial.[11]

The most dramatic courtroom scenes took place during the Luciano trail, a prosecution that shared the front pages of New York newspapers in early April 1919 with wire stories from Paris about efforts to conclude a peace treaty for the recently ended Great War. The hapless motorman, carefully coached by his BRT defense team, described the events leading up to the accident in a way that made it sound as if he had followed BRT procedures to the letter. "Then I started down toward the Consumers' Park station and expected to receive three bells to stop there. None were rung," Luciano claimed. "I shut off the power and started to coast. The train jumped ahead so fast that I put on the air [brakes], but they would not hold. Then I applied the emergency [brake], and that would not hold and I reversed my power. The next thing I knew we were crashing."[12]

Although this testimony is a textbook-perfect rendition of what Luciano should have done, it is not even remotely consistent with hard evidence the BRT itself had assembled after it took charge of the train on Sunday, November 3, 1918. Tests performed at that time indicated that the train's conventional braking system was in proper working order, the emergency brakes were never applied, and circuits on all three power cars were set in a Brighton Beach–bound orientation—meaning that no reverse power had been applied.[13]

Why the prosecution failed to use this information more effectively to rebut Luciano's testimony is yet another mystery. The PSC was aware of the BRT's tests, and their own staff of engineers went over the train carefully as early as Saturday, November 2, even before BRT personnel were permitted back into the tunnel. There is evidence in the reports and minutes of PSC meetings that the commission forwarded its documents to the prosecuting attorney for his use.[14] Furthermore, a PSC engineer by the name of Joseph Connor who participated in the BRT's own evaluations, was called as a state's witness at the Luciano trial.[15]

The prosecution shifted gears between the earlier Blewitt trial and the Luciano trial. They had portrayed Blewitt as an agent of the BRT, saying that he and the company were criminally at fault in allowing an unqualified motorman—Edward Luciano—to operate the fatal train. The prosecutors took great pains to convince the Blewitt jury that Luciano was completely unqualified. A month later when Luciano was the defendant, his own lack of motorman's qualifications would have represented a better defense strategy than one for the prosecution. Consequently, the state built its case around what it called gross carelessness on Luciano's part, avoiding any discussion of his training and competence. "It doesn't make a particle of difference whether this man was qualified or unqualified," said Herbert Warbasse, the assistant district attorney who handled the Luciano trial.[16]

Luciano took the stand in his own defense. On two different occasions while under direct examination by his attorney, he broke down in tears and Judge Seeger was forced to suspend the proceedings so Luciano could compose himself. Warbasse objected forcefully to this, claiming it was all contrived and deliberate; he was promptly overruled.

Emotions ran high throughout the Luciano trial. When Lewis Smith summarized for the defense before the case was handed to the jury for deliberation, the sometime Nassau County judge said this: "I don't care what you think of the BRT. All I ask is don't cast the sins of the company, if there are any, upon that boy." As Smith concluded his summation, Luciano's wife Josephine entered the courtroom together with the couple's only surviving child, two-year-old Geraldine. The little girl saw her father and cried out, "Papa."[17]

The jury's deliberations took 4 hours and 49 minutes. Before casting the third and final tally that resulted in Luciano's acquittal, the jury had earlier voted to reject the prosecution's case by counts of 9 to 3 and 11 to 1. One of the jurors later said that the state failed to demonstrate that brake failure did not cause the accident.[18]

Documents among the Hylan papers in the Archives of the City of New York tell a story of a very disjointed effort at prosecution, with the principal motivation being to wage war against the higher officials of the BRT. One city attorney wrote a lengthy memorandum explaining why, in his professional opinion, corporate officers of a railway company could not be held criminally liable for an accident such as the Malbone Street Wreck. His views were disregarded, and the thrust of the prosecution's efforts continued to be an attempt to place blame for the tragedy on high-level company officials.[19]

Hylan and Lewis worked closely on the case, exchanging many memoranda. One is left to conclude that it was Hylan's fury over the very concept of privately operated mass transit in New York that dictated the course of the prosecution—namely, an all-out effort to discredit the highest corporate officers of the BRT, rather than a careful evaluation of the facts in the case and an effort to identify specific actions of a clear and provable criminal nature.

For example, prosecutors focused a good deal of attention on questions of design. Was the newly built curve into the tunnel at the foot of the hill too sharp by railway and rapid transit standards? While it was a sharp curve, it was certainly no sharper than many others being incorporated into various portions of the BRT's new Dual Subway Contracts lines, although its position at the end of a downhill grade with no signals to monitor the speed of approaching trains was a little out of the ordinary. However, raising questions of design ensured that high-level executives of the BRT would be forced to answer such charges. This is what led to the indictment against William Menden, the company's chief engineer.

Other documents among the Hylan Papers tell of a prosecution that failed to familiarize itself with even the rudiments of electric railway operation, despite the fact that the prosecution retained several railway experts for technical assistance and advice.[20] There was some discussion of the BRT's normal training and certification procedures for motormen, for instance, but prosecutors made little effort to document them carefully and then probe as to why these policies were so utterly ignored on November 1. The prosecution remained an unfocused effort that failed to distinguish the important from the trivial. More than adequate documentary evidence was available to disprove Luciano's account of the trip down Crown Heights, but the prosecution never effectively developed it.

Of the various efforts to levy criminal charges following the Malbone Street Wreck, at least this can be said: no innocent people were ever sent to prison. Table 5 identifies all the criminal prosecutions undertaken in the wake of the Malbone Street Wreck.

The final arena for seeking justice in the aftermath of the Malbone

TABLE 5: CRIMINAL PROSECUTIONS FOLLOWING THE MALBONE STREET WRECK

Date	Action	Presiding Judge
March 18, 1919	Blewitt acquitted	Seeger
April 4, 1919	Luciano acquitted	Seeger
December 18, 1919	Dempsey trial ended in a hung jury	Kapper
January 26, 1920	Menden trial ended in directed verdict of acquittal	Callaghan
April 14, 1920	Second Dempsey trial ended in acquittal	Scudder
January 17, 1921	On motion of District Attorney Lewis, all remaining indictments dismissed	Lazansky

Street Wreck was that of civil liability. The old expression "justice delayed is justice denied" may well be the perfect description of the final monetary settlements reached for what happened on the Brighton Beach Line on the evening of November 1, 1918. Other than cases where survivors, or next of kin, sold their right of claim against the BRT to some third party—and, supposedly, this was not uncommon—no victims received so much as one thin dime in settlement for almost five years.

The delay can be explained by a series of events that took place during the final week of 1918. Anxious meetings and urgent conferences were held in various Manhattan board rooms, law offices, and judicial chambers. At issue was the refinancing of a critical BRT 7 percent note for $57 million that would fall due on January 1, 1919, but which the traction company was unable to meet. Late on the evening of December 31, Federal Judge Julius M. Mayer concluded that the troubled BRT was incapable of resolving its financial problems without judicial intervention. Acting on a petition filed earlier by the Westinghouse Electric and Manufacturing Company to force payment of certain past-due obligations, Judge Mayer placed the BRT under receivership and appointed former U.S. Secretary of War Lindley M. Garrison as trustee.[21] Garrison was not unfamiliar with the BRT. He was the man who the BRT itself had earlier designated as its arbitrator in a dispute with the PSC over whether costs arising out of the Malbone Street Wreck were to be regarded as "operating expenses" under the terms of the Dual Subway Contracts.

Judge Mayer's temporary order of December 31 was to be returned on January 2; it was promptly made permanent. Garrison immediately sought to relieve any anxiety over the settlement of claims arising out of the November 1 accident and promised that he would "see that everything humanly possible is done to see that funds are available to pay all just claims growing out of the Malbone Street accident."[22] His assurances, however, proved to be empty promises. The action of December 31, 1918, put all Malbone Street claims under protection of the court; they would not be settled until the receivership was discharged.

Another piece of incorrect Malbone Street folklore—perhaps the one that has been repeated more often than any other—is that the Malbone Street Wreck itself caused the BRT's bankruptcy. Although the accident certainly did not benefit the company's overall financial position, the extent of the BRT's other debts was so enormous and its financial prospects were so bleak that the Malbone Street Wreck—from the perspective of dollars alone—was simply not that significant. If there had never been a Malbone Street Wreck, the BRT would have entered receivership exactly when and as it did. Within days of the accident, insurance experts were quietly predicting that the company's liability exposure for the events of November 1 would amount to about $2 million.[23] (In fact, it turned out to be several hundred thousand dollars less.) Given all the company's other debts and deferred obligations, an additional $2 million was simply not a sufficient sum to cause bankruptcy.

Mayor Hylan reacted to the BRT receivership by calling on newly elected Governor Smith to put the entire PSC under receivership, as well.[24] Failing that, Hylan directed the city's corporation counsel to petition Judge Mayer to establish coreceivers for the troubled BRT. To protect the city's interest in the BRT, the petition requested that New York City Comptroller, Charles L. Craig, be named to serve as a receiver along with Garrison.[25] The city's petition was rejected.

Some civil trials were held and out-of-court settlements reached between victims and the BRT in the months following the accident. But no money changed hands; these merely established liability and set a dollar figure for damages. Obtaining real dollars had to wait for the discharge of the receivership; attorneys counseled their clients to be patient. Eventually even the lawyers lost their patience. In February 1921, a group of 40 attorneys who represented Malbone Street victims formed the Tort Creditors' Legislative Protective Association, whose purpose was to expedite the settlement of claims pending against the BRT. Lindley Garrison, who earlier expressed the hope that Malbone Street claims could be swiftly settled despite the receivership, soon adopted the position that because "damage claims arising out of the Malbone Street accident were prior to the receivership . . . the receiver has no funds which in any way could possibly be paid for such damages."[26]

It was not until mid-1923 that the parties involved reached an agreement that allowed the receivership to end and a successor company to continue the work of the BRT. Then, and only then, did victims of the Malbone Street Wreck receive monetary compensation. For cases that had not yet been adjudicated, the bankruptcy court had earlier appointed Philip J. McCook to serve as "special master" and take evidence from individual claimants and recommend final awards to Judge Mayer, who was supervising the overall bankruptcy proceedings.[27]

The BRT did not contest liability with respect to the accident; in other words, the company acknowledged it was at fault. But the company was very aggressive in contesting facts associated with individual injury claims, and hence the extent of the settlements being sought. As relatively minor cases of modest injuries came before the court-appointed special master seeking minimal awards—perhaps the mere recovery of a few days' lost wages—the BRT countered with evidence gathered by special agents and physicians who had visited the homes of Malbone Street victims, usually unannounced. These agents then testified that a given individual could have returned to work earlier, or that a person was up and walking around and not bedridden as claimed, and therefore the amount sought should be lowered. It usually was. (See appendix D for a partial listing of civil settlements.)

Finally everything was settled. In June 1923 a new company, the Brooklyn-Manhattan Transit Corporation, purchased the assets of the BRT, refinanced its debt, and took over its operations.[28] Three months later, as part of the court-approved plan that involved refinancing $102.8 million of back debt and securities of the BRT, plus the provision of $26 million in new capital, the company deposited $1.6 million in a special account at the Chase National Bank in New York to pay off Malbone Street claims.[29] The money was then allocated into separate, non-interest-bearing accounts in appropriate amounts for each of the claimants. All were notified that the company's liability for the events of November 1, 1918, was now considered a closed matter.

NOTES

1. The police station and magistrate's court at 35 Snyder Avenue (between Flatbush and Bedford avenues) is itself a historic piece of Brooklyn architecture. Built in 1875 as a town hall for the town of Flatbush, the building is today used by the city's board of education and is listed on the National Register of Historic Places. See William L. Lebovich, *America's City Halls* (Washington, D.C.: The Preservation Press, 1984), 73.

2. For his own views on this matter, see *Mayor Hylan of New York; An Autobiography* (New York: Rotary Press, 1922), 23–5. This is not a book-length autobiography but a self-serving pamphlet. However, there can be no doubt it accurately reflects Hylan's own thoughts.

3. For the text of bitter correspondence between the PSC and Hylan, see *New York Journal* (November 2, 1918), 3; *New York Times* (November 4, 1918), 2.

4. See *Brooklyn Eagle* (December 11, 1918), 1.

5. For extended excerpts from these proceedings, see *Brooklyn Eagle* (December 11, 1918), 2.

6. Citation of all indictments may be found in handwritten record books of the Kings County Supreme Court for Friday, December 20, 1918. Luciano is identified in the indictment as "Edward Luciano, alias Anthony Lewis."

7. See "BRT Takes Canvass," *Electric Railway Journal* 52 (December 28, 1918): 1150.

8. Several such letters may be found among the John Francis Hylan Papers. See Hylan Papers, box 197, folders 10 and 11, Archives of the City of New York, New York.

9. For the full text of Callaghan's change of venue order, see *People v. Williams et al.*, New York Supreme Court, Special Term for Motions, Kings County (January 29, 1919), 883–90.

10. Edward Erskine Porter, 25 years old when he was killed, graduated from Brooklyn Polytechnic Institute and Williams College and worked in Manhattan in the bond department of Harris, Forbes and Company. He was the son of a noted Brooklyn real estate man, David Porter. Young Porter and his wife, the former Eloise Bennett Knox of Savannah, Georgia, lived at 307 Caton Avenue, near East Third Street, in Brooklyn. The couple's only child was born three weeks before the Malbone Street Wreck. Porter is buried in Brooklyn's Greenwood Cemetery. Thomas Gilfeather, the son of Irish immigrants, was 34 years old at the time of his death and lived in Brooklyn at 388 East 49th Street, near Linden Boulevard. He was in the trucking business at 109 West 24th Street in Manhattan and was survived by his wife, Hortense Boyle Rosbotham Gilfeather, and a daughter, Anna. Gilfeather is buried in Brooklyn's Holy Cross Cemetery.

11. "I deem it a practical impossibility to secure conviction on the trial of the other indictments," said District Attorney Lewis. See *New York Times* (January 18, 1921), 6.

12. *New York Herald* (April 4, 1919), 3.

13. On November 20, 1918, J. R. Ellicott of the Westinghouse Traction Brake Company sent a six-page report to W. G. Gove, the BRT's superintendent of equipment, detailing tests his company performed on the train

shortly after the wreck. This report concluded that the braking system was in perfect working order and that an emergency brake application was not made prior to the crash. In addition, a companion report to Gove from the Carnegie Steel Company provided detailed information on the condition of the train's wheels; no "flat spots" were found, something that would be almost impossible had an emergency brake application been made. (In fact, the train's wheels were in such good condition as to cast doubt on the characterization of Luciano's train operation earlier in the trip as erratic and irresponsible. Had the trip been as bad as some observers claimed it to be, Luciano likely would have applied the emergency brake earlier to avoid overshooting stations.) Finally, an internal BRT memorandum to Gove dated November 11, 1918, from G. J. McDonough, foreman of the company's Southern Division Inspection and Overhaul Shop, presented additional findings from a review of the wrecked train; McDonough found that the motors were not put into reverse before the crash. Gove forwarded all of these reports to George E. Yoemans, the company's chief counsel, on November 26, 1918. I obtained copies of these documents from the personal collection of Donald W. Harold.

14. See Public Service Commission for the First District, *Proceedings;* item 3152 (November 8, 1918), 1647.

15. *Brooklyn Eagle* (April 2, 1919), 1, 3.

16. *Brooklyn Times* (April 1, 1919), 1.

17. *New York Herald* (April 5, 1919), 1.

18. For a brief account of the deliberations of the Luciano jury, see *New York Herald* (April 5, 1919), 1.

19. The four-page memo, which was written by assistant corporation counsel James A. Donnelly, argues: "I do not believe any of the defendants named in the information can be held criminally responsible as directors, unless it can be shown that the acts or omissions complained of are by statute made a crime." See "Transit Disaster," Hylan Papers, box 197, folder 10, Archives of the City of New York.

20. One railway expert retained by Mayor Hylan who worked with District Attorney Lewis was a man by the name of E. C. M. Rand. Various letters written by Rand may be found in "Transit Disaster," Hylan Papers.

21. *New York Times* (January 1, 1919), 1.

22. *New York Times* (January 4, 1919), 1.

23. *Brooklyn Eagle* (November 3, 1918), 3.

24. *New York Times* (January 2, 1919), 1, 14.

25. *New York Times* (January 3, 1919), 1.

26. *New York Times* (March 20, 1921), sec. II, p. 1.

27. For further information on the BRT during the period of receivership, see U.S. District Court, Consolidated Cause in Equity No. 15–345

(Westinghouse Electric and Manufacturing Company, Plaintiff, against Brooklyn Rapid Transit Company, New York Municipal Railway Corporation and New York Consolidated Railroad Company, Defendants), Justice Julius M. Mayer. Available in the National Archives, New York. (There are more than 2,000 entries in two different docket books, volumes 15 and 19. Exhibits and backup material are contained in approximately 50 archival boxes.)

28. See "The Plan to Reorganize the BRT System," *BRT Monthly* (May 1923): 12–3. Among the documents contained in the court file of the BRT bankruptcy is a detailed report entitled "Adoption and Approval of Plan" that provides more complete details of the reorganization. (U.S. District Court, dockets 15 and 19, carton 679, National Archives, New York). One element of the BRT that did not emerge from receivership in 1923 to become part of the Brooklyn-Manhattan Transit Corporation was the Brighton Beach Hotel. Built by the Brooklyn, Flatbush and Coney Island Railroad in 1878, it remained associated with the Brighton Beach Line until the reorganization of 1923, when it was liquidated. Shortly thereafter, the old turreted wooden building that had been hauled inland by six of the railroad's steam locomotives in 1888 was torn down and apartment houses soon rose on the site. For those familiar with Brighton Beach today, the place where the Brighton Beach Hotel once stood is between Brighton Beach Avenue and the ocean to the west of Coney Island Avenue. See *New York Times* (March 6, 1923), 6.

29. See *New York Times* (July 20, 1923), 18; *New York Times* (July 29, 1923), sec. I, pt. 2, p. 5; *New York Times* (September 15, 1923), 14.

EPILOGUE

The Brooklyn-Manhattan Transit Corporation, the BMT—successor company of the BRT—was not to enjoy a long life. In 1940 it was sold to the municipal government and became the BMT division of the city's board of transportation.[1] The recommendation made by a committee of the American Electric Railway Association to all U.S. public transit companies on the very day of the Malbone Street Wreck—and what John Francis Hylan had championed during his eight years in City Hall—was becoming accepted practice in New York and throughout the United States. The public sector of subsidy and service was replacing the private sector of risk and profit as the principal agent in the provision of urban mass transportation.

The BMT surrendered its assets and mass transit responsibilities to the city's board of transportation at the stroke of midnight on June 2, 1940. Although the corporation no longer operated any trains, trolley cars, or buses after the handover, certain business details to finalize the transaction required further attention and the BMT remained an active corporate entity. Ironically, it was on November 1, 1941—the 23rd anniversary of the Malbone Street Wreck—when the *New York Times* reported that the New York Stock Exchange had notified its members that the BMT was officially and permanently dissolved.[2]

As to the Brighton Beach Line, the new Flatbush Avenue tunnel that was incomplete and under construction on November 1, 1918, was opened for service on Sunday, August 1, 1920. Since that day, the Brighton Beach Line has been linked with the BRT/BMT subway network that was built under the terms of the Dual Subway Contracts; the extension up and over Crown Heights no longer serves as the Brighton Beach Line's connection with downtown Brooklyn and Manhattan. The connection with the Fulton Street elevated train at Franklin and Fulton was severed, and the old line over Crown Heights was turned into a mere shuttle service linking Prospect Park and Franklin Avenue; it was later assigned its own route number in a new BMT service identification system. The Franklin Avenue shuttle, as the service has since been called, was identified as the BMT's number 7 line. In today's letter-code system, the designation is a generic S, for shuttle.

The Franklin Avenue shuttle underwent somewhat of a renaissance. In 1924 the line was upgraded to permit the operation of six-car, steel subway trains, and in the summertime—when heavy seasonal crowds headed for the beaches—the BMT operated a service pattern that was reminiscent of the days of the Brooklyn, Flatbush and Coney Island Railroad.[3] Direct express service from Franklin and Fulton to Coney Island continued through the summer of 1954.

In the 1920s transportation officials talked of a possible major new role for the Franklin Avenue shuttle; it would be extended beyond Fulton Street, run across central Brooklyn, and link up with other BRT/BMT lines in Long Island City. Such plans never got beyond the talking stage, however.

In the late 1950s, the city made an operational change in the Franklin Avenue shuttle, and trains no longer used the infamous curve at the foot of the hill. The change had nothing to do with the curve itself; it was adopted to avoid delays caused by shuttle trains using in-service trackage of the Brighton Beach Line south of Prospect Park station to change ends and reverse direction.

A crossover switch was installed connecting northbound and southbound tracks between the tunnel portal and the Washington Avenue overpass, and shuttle trains could arrive at and depart from the northbound platform at Prospect Park. The curve into the Malbone Street tunnel was left in place, the trackage remained operational, and a few trains each day used the older route as they were being taken out of service after the morning or evening rush hour. But as a general rule, the infamous Malbone Street curve was no longer routinely used in passenger service (see map 5 for a view of today's track layout at the Prospect Park Station).

It was almost a quarter-century after municipal transportation officials implemented this new operating protocol when a relatively minor accident and derailment evoked memories of November 1, 1918. On December 1, 1974, a southbound shuttle train was approaching the tunnel portal en route from Franklin Avenue when it derailed on the crossover and smashed into the face of the same

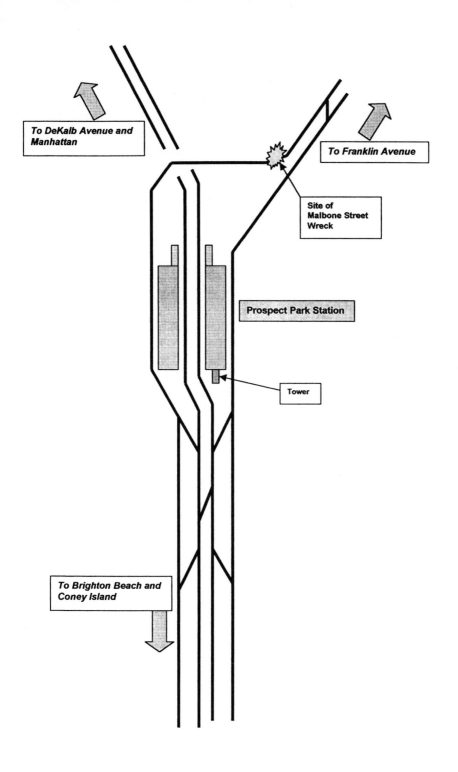

To DeKalb Avenue and Manhattan

To Franklin Avenue

Site of Malbone Street Wreck

Prospect Park Station

Tower

To Brighton Beach and Coney Island

tunnel portal that BRT car 100 had hit with such force in 1918. Because time signals now limit the speed of trains coming down the hill from Crown Heights, the 1974 derailment was more of an inconvenience than a tragedy; it resulted in some injuries but no fatalities. As was the case in 1918, rescue forces from the New York Fire Department again had to set up ladders from street level down to track level.

The Fulton Street elevated line that once provided Brighton Beach Line trains access to downtown Brooklyn and Manhattan no longer exists. It was abandoned with the sale of the BMT to the city of New York in 1940 and torn down, but that does not mean Fulton Street is bereft of rapid transit service. A new high-speed, four-track subway line had earlier been constructed under Fulton Street as part of the city's Independent Subway System, and passengers could freely transfer between the new subway and the old shuttle at Franklin and Fulton.

In the 1980s, New York City Transit suggested abandoning the Franklin Avenue shuttle entirely, since by New York standards the route did not carry that many passengers—10,000 or so a day—and many elements of the line had seriously deteriorated. The original tunnel under Empire Boulevard/Malbone Street, for instance, required the installation of temporary wooden supports to preserve its structural integrity, and stations along the line were equally shabby. Improved bus service along nearby Franklin Avenue, the Transit Authority claimed, could substitute for the old rail line.

Community members quickly rallied to oppose this proposal. Although the Dean Street station was permanently closed in 1995, rapid transit service on the Franklin Avenue shuttle was suspended for several months in 1998 to permit a $74 million rebuilding of the entire line. This railway, which operated its first train in August 1878, appears to have more good years ahead.

The Brotherhood of Locomotive Engineers never became a major bargaining agent for New York transit workers. In the years after 1918, other unions of national scope picked up the cause of organizing subway workers. For instance, during the Luciano trial in the spring of 1919, Lindley Garrison—the BRT's court-appointed receiver—rebuffed a bid by the Amalgamated Association of Street and Electric Railway Workers to be designated a formal bargaining agent for the company's workers. However, unionism was a powerful force; by the time the BMT was sold to the city government in 1940, not only were its workers "allowed" to join independent trade unions, but a union shop prevailed among the ranks.[4]

Edward Luciano resigned from the BRT shortly after his acquittal and began a new career in real estate. Sometime in 1919, the Luciano family moved from 160 34th Street to a new apartment a block away on 33rd Street. Luciano later testified at the second Dempsey trial, but after that he faded from the scene and little is known about him. It is said that he lived a long life. According to some rumors, he later made his home someplace on Long Island; others claim that he moved to upstate New York. It is said that the events of that awful November evening left a permanent scar on the man. Small wonder.

The unmarked grave in Brooklyn's Holy Cross Cemetery where Luciano's two young daughters were buried—one in late October 1918, less than a week before the Malbone Street Wreck, the other in 1914—is not where he and his wife are interred. This fact gives credibility to the reports that he moved away from Brooklyn. In the 1920 U.S. Census, the most recent federal enumeration whose raw data are available for study, the man who was indicted and tried as Edward Luciano reported his name as Anthony Lewis. Called Lewis before the Malbone Street Wreck, indicted and tried after the tragedy as Luciano, the man presumably reverted to Lewis for the remainder of his days. One must hope that he eventually found a measure of peace.

With respect to the executives who were indicted, William Menden was to enjoy further productive years with the BRT and the BMT. A native of Evansville, Indiana, who held a civil engineering degree from Rose Polytechnic Institute in Terre Haute and who came to the BRT in 1905 after an earlier stint with the elevated railways of Chicago, he was named general manager during the period of the BRT's receivership. After the reorganization in 1923, he became the BMT's first and only president. He served in that capacity until the municipal takeover in 1940. He died in 1949 at the age of 79.[5]

Former BRT president Timothy Williams, the ex-newspaper man who had been one of the founding directors of the BRT in 1896, tendered his resignation to the trustee in bankruptcy in January 1920, 14 months after the Malbone Street Wreck. He retired to his home in the West Neck section of Huntington, Long Island, although he sometimes performed tasks for the trustee in the capacity of a consultant. Williams died in Brooklyn in 1930 at the age of 67.[6]

It was John Dempsey, 39 years old in 1918 and with no formal education beyond grammar school, whose post-Malbone career was the most unusual of all the BRT officials associated with the tragedy. He resigned from the BRT on September 1, 1919, during the period of receivership. He then accepted an executive position with the R. E. Seamans Company, a firm that was active in the rapidly expanding field of petroleum and petroleum products. The Seamans office in New York was located in the Flatiron Building at Broadway and West 23rd Street. Dempsey's career in the oil business eventually took him to the southwestern part of the United States and residence in Santa Fe, New Mexico. There, beginning in 1935, Dempsey was elected to seven terms in the U.S. House of Representatives and one as governor of New Mexico. Dempsey also held two appointed positions in the Roosevelt administration during the early years of the Second World War. He died in 1958 at the age of 79. Like his former nemesis Mayor Hylan, Dempsey conducted his political career as a member of the Democratic Party.[7]

John Francis Hylan, initially elected to a four-year term as mayor in 1917, was reelected in 1921 with a larger plurality than in any New York mayoral election since the municipal amalgamation of 1898. The principal issue that generated this landslide victory was Hylan's staunch opposition to subway fare increases proposed by the Interborough Rapid Transit Company and the BRT. During his second term, Hylan convinced state lawmakers in Albany to enact legislation that resulted in the construction of the city's third subway system—a completely municipally owned and municipally operated network known as the Independent Subway System. By the time the new subway system's first line opened for revenue service in 1932, Hylan was no longer mayor and was serving as a justice in children's court in Queens. He died at his home in Forest Hills in his 68th year on January 12, 1936.[8]

As for Malbone Street, because of its association with the tragic events of November 1, 1918, the street was eventually renamed Empire Boulevard; it has remained so ever since. But as has been seen so often throughout the account of the Malbone Street Wreck, a degree of qualification must be added even to this seemingly simple fact.

In the 19th century, before Brooklyn's current urban street grid was established, there was an earlier Malbone Street that followed a slightly different alignment than the broad and straight thoroughfare that was renamed Empire Boulevard after the accident. Strangely, a vestigial element of the old Malbone Street running at an odd angle for just a few blocks remains a public way in Brooklyn to this day. It is a short walk east from the scene of the accident, a little beyond what was once the right field wall of Ebbets Field. This street is still called Malbone Street.

Brooklyn residents who go about their daily business today and ride bicycles and push baby carriages and deliver mail under contemporary green and white New York City street signs that read "Malbone St." are probably unaware of what unspeakable horror such a simple name once conveyed. Perhaps it is just as well.

NOTES

1. Between 1940 and 1953, public ownership and operation of the BMT and Interborough Rapid Transit Company was through a conventional department of the municipal government, the board of transportation. In 1953, a new agency, the New York City Transit Authority, was created by the state legislature to assume responsibility for operating the city's subway system.

2. *New York Times* (November 1, 1941), 22.

3. For information about the changes that were made on the Franklin Avenue shuttle, see "Providing Better Transit for the Beach Traffic," *BMT Monthly* (May 1924): 2–3.

4. For an extremely detailed account of the rise of organized labor on the New York mass transit scene, particularly in the years before and after the Malbone Street Wreck, see James J. McGinley, *Labor Relations in the New York Rapid Transit Systems, 1904–1944* (New York: King's Crown, 1949).

5. See "William S. Menden Elected President," *BMT Monthly* (August 1923): 2. See also *New York Times* (September 28, 1949), 27.

6. See "Col. Williams Leaves BRT after Quarter Century of Service," *BRT Monthly* (January 1920): 3–4. See also *New York Times* (June 4, 1930), 1, 27.

7. For general information on John Dempsey's career with the BRT, see

"J. J. Dempsey Resigns from BRT," *BRT Monthly* (August 1919): 3, 22. I wrote to the official archivist of the state of New Mexico and inquired if any documents among Governor Dempsey's papers might relate to the Malbone Street Wreck. The answer was that none did.

8. *New York Times* (January 12, 1936), 1, 21.

APPENDIX A
The Malbone Street Wreck and Other Disasters

Although it may seem insensitive to characterize and compare disasters solely in terms of the fatal casualties they produced, such a comparison represents a means for understanding the larger context of the Malbone Street Wreck.

TABLE A.1.: THE THREE WORST DISASTERS IN BROOKLYN HISTORY

Date	Incident	Fatal Injuries
Dec. 5, 1876	Fire in Brooklyn Theatre on Fulton Street	295
Dec. 16, 1960	Airliner crash in Park Slope[a]	95
Nov. 1, 1918	Malbone Street Wreck[b]	93

[a] On December 16, 1960, a United Airlines DC-8 en route from Chicago to Idlewild Airport collided over Staten Island with a Trans World Airlines Constellation en route from Dayton, Ohio, to La Guardia Airport. The DC-8 crashed in Brooklyn, the Constellation in Staten Island. Fatal injuries were as follows: 39 aboard the Constellation, 89 aboard the DC-8, 6 on the ground in Brooklyn.
[b] See text for issues associated with the actual number of fatal injuries in the Malbone Street Wreck.

TABLE A.2: THE TEN WORST U.S. RAILWAY DISASTERS

Date	Location	Fatal Injuries
Jul. 9, 1918	Nashville, Tennessee	101
Aug. 7, 1904	Eden, Colorado	96
Mar. 1, 1910	Wellington, Washington	96
Nov. 1, 1918	Malbone Street Wreck[a]	93

Dec. 29, 1876	Ashtabula, Ohio	92
Feb. 6, 1951	Woodbridge, New Jersey	84
Aug. 10, 1887	Chatsworth, Illinois	81
Sept. 6, 1943	Philadelphia, Pennsylvania	79
Nov. 22, 1950	Richmond Hill, New York	79
Dec. 16, 1943	Near Rennert, North Carolina	72

[a] See text for issues associated with the actual number of fatal injuries in the Malbone Street Wreck.

TABLE A.3: THE TEN WORST DISASTERS IN METROPOLITAN NEW YORK

Date	Incident	Fatal Injuries
June 16, 1904	Fire aboard steamboat *General Slocum*	1,030
June 30, 1900	Hoboken dock fire	329
Dec. 5, 1876	Brooklyn Theatre fire	295
Mar. 25, 1911	Triangle Shirtwaist Company fire	145
Dec. 16, 1960	Crash of two airliners following mid-air collision[a]	134
June 24, 1975	Airliner crash at John F. Kennedy Airport	113
Mar. 1, 1962	Airliner crash in Jamaica Bay	95
Nov. 1, 1918	Malbone Street Wreck[b]	93
Feb. 6, 1951	Commuter train derailment in Woodbridge, New Jersey	84
Nov. 22, 1950	Two commuter trains collide in Richmond Hill, New York	79

[a] On December 16, 1960, a United Airlines DC-8 en route from Chicago to Idlewild Airport collided over Staten Island with a Trans World Airlines Constellation en route from Dayton, Ohio, to La Guardia Airport. The DC-8 crashed in Brooklyn, the Constellation in Staten Island. Fatal injuries were as follows: 39 aboard the Constellation, 89 aboard the DC-8, 6 on the ground in Brooklyn.

[b] See text for issues associated with the actual number of fatal injuries in the Malbone Street Wreck.

APPENDIX B

The Fatal Trip of November 1, 1918: A Reconstructed Schedule

INBOUND

Lv. Kings Highway Yard	5:15 P.M.
(surface operation via Culver Line)	
Lv. Kings Highway Station	5:17 P.M.
Lv. Avenue P	5:19 P.M.
Lv. Avenue N	5:21 P.M.
Lv. 22nd Avenue	5:23 P.M.
Lv. Parkville	5:26 P.M.
Lv. 18th Avenue	5:28 P.M.
Lv. Kensington	5:31 P.M.
Lv. 16th Avenue	5:33 P.M.
Lv. 13th Avenue	5:36 P.M.
Lv. Fort Hamilton Avenue	5:37 P.M.
Lv. Ninth Avenue	5:39 P.M.
Lv. Eighth Avenue	5:41 P.M.
Lv. 36th Street	5:43 P.M.
(elevated operation via Fifth Avenue Line)	
Lv. 25th Street	5:45 P.M.
Lv. 20th Street	5:46 P.M.
Lv. 16th Street	5:47 P.M.
Lv. 9th Street	5:49 P.M.
Lv. 3d Street	5:50 P.M.
Lv. Union Street	5:51 P.M.
Lv. St. Marks Avenue	5:52 P.M.
Lv. Atlantic Avenue	5:54 P.M.
Lv. Fulton Street	5:56 P.M.

Lv. Bridge Street .... 5:58 P.M.
     (elevated operation via Myrtle Avenue Line)
Lv. Sands Street (via Brooklyn Bridge) .... 5:59 P.M.
Ar. Park Row .... 6:08 P.M.

OUTBOUND

Lv. Park Row (via Brooklyn Bridge) .... 6:14 P.M.
Lv. Sands Street .... 6:19 P.M.
     (elevated operation via Fulton Street Line)
Lv. Court Street .... 6:21 P.M.
Lv. Boerum Place .... 6:22 P.M.
Lv. Elm/Duffield .... 6:23 P.M.
Lv. Flatbush Avenue .... 6:24 P.M.
Lv. Lafayette Avenue .... 6:26 P.M.
Lv. Cumberland Street .... 6:27 P.M.
Lv. Vanderbilt Avenue .... 6:28 P.M.
Lv. Grand Avenue .... 6:29 P.M.
Ar. Franklin Avenue (Fulton Street Line platform) .... 6:30 P.M.
Lv. Franklin Avenue (Brighton Beach Line platform) .... 6:38 P.M.
     (elevated and at grade operation via Brighton Beach Line)
Lv. Dean Street .... 6:39 P.M.
Lv. Park Place .... 6:40 P.M.
—   Malbone Street Wreck .... 6:42 P.M.

Source: Schedule has been established from several known times, including the
time of the accident; times at intermediate stations have been estimated from BRT
schedules.

APPENDIX C

Fatally Injured Passengers in the Malbone Street Wreck

TABLE C.1: The 93 Persons Fatally Injured in the Malbone Street Wreck

Name	Age	Brooklyn Address
1. Alexander, James	19	747 Fenmore St.
2. Alfaro, Pascual F.	26	160 Robinson St.
3. Amerin, Ada F.[a]	40	Riverside Dr. and 135th St., Manhattan
4. Arena, Charles[b]	39	186 Lefferts Ave.
5. Arena, Mabel[b]	41	186 Lefferts Ave.
6. Barcan, Etta	32	1145 E. 14th St.
7. Bechtold, Elsie M.	20	362 E. 9th St.
8. Berkowitz, Herman	39	2927 2nd Street
9. Bogen, David	27	97 Kenmore Pl.
10. Borcino, Edward Snyder	46	42 Henry St.
11. Borden, Helen	24	1011 Ocean Ave.
12. Brunswick, David	70	847 E. 10th St.
13. Burton, Violet	14	1458 E. 17th St.
14. Cleary, Margaret T.	18	318 Parkside Ave.
15. Clifford, Louise M.	30	485 Argyle Rd.
16. Coady, Emily	58	682 Argyle Rd.
17. Condra, Louise	23	413 Ave. C West
18. Cooper, Margaret[a, c]	64	Detroit, Michigan
19. Cuicotta, Rose	34	1935 E. 9th St.
20. Edholm, Alvera S.	30	391 Ocean Ave.
21. Enggren, John William	47	37 E. 10th St.
22. Flahive, James F.	32	297 E. 38th St.
23. Fleming, Catherine	35	9 E. 10th St.
24. Gardner, Marian E.	52	347 Lincoln Rd.
25. Gilbert, Michael[d]	26	1519 E. 18th St.

26.	Gilfeather, Thomas F.[e]	34	388 E. 49th St.
27.	Gillen, Harry Peter	26	1634 E. 13th St.
28.	Givnan, Thomas J.	28	1601 Voorhees Ave.
29.	Halloran, James J.	36	Ave. Z and E. 38th St.
30.	Haltorf, Theodore F.	59	984 E. 18th St.
31.	Harris, Gertrude M.	25	810 Ave. W
32.	Hennion, Emilienne	24	85 Lennox St.
33.	Holmes, George W.	35	661 Westminster Rd.
34.	Hopkins, Louis L.	48	2131 Bedford Ave.
35.	Jackowitz, Sophie	22	4301 Church Ave.
36.	Johansen, Anna	48	1615 Emmons Ave.
37.	Judd, Frank A.	45	268 Beaumont St.
38.	Kempf, Christina	41	203 Parkside Ave.
39.	Kerr, David Patton	33	1448 35th St.
40.	Kinsie, Benjamin A.	49	79 Haven Ave.
41.	Kirchhoff, Clara	35	877 E. 15th St.
42.	Larson, Henry A.	48	713 Ave. W
43.	Lee, Frederick Walter	17	324 Parkside Ave.
44.	Lerner, Nathan	41	1585 President St.
45.	Lombard, Henry L.	41	1919 E. 18th St.
46.	Love, Bessie	19	90 St. Marks Pl.
47.	Lovering, Frank J.	55	1025 E. 15th St.
48.	Lyons, Carolyn	37	1616 Ave. H
49.	Maier, Joseph I.	49	204 Midwood St.
50.	Malamud, Abraham	54	602 E. 16th St.
51.	Maloney, Lillian M.	26	176 Lefferts Ave.
52.	Matlock, Ethel M.	20	325 E. 21st St.
53.	McCormack, Grace F.	17	1404 Cortelyou Rd.
54.	McMillan, Garnet E.[a, f]	28	· Charleston, South Carolina
55.	Meehan, Helen	26	348 Eastern Pkwy.
56.	Metzger, Ira Harrison	28	876 E. 14th St.
57.	Minton, Frederick F.	54	398 E. 18th St.
58.	Munn, Sadie L.	42	25 Rugby Rd.
59.	Murphy, Grace	32	1927 Homecrest Ave.
60.	Mussen, Silas Wright	27	402 Ocean Ave.
61.	Nagle, Richard	43	2124 E. 4th St.
62.	Palmedo, Alexander M.	52	430 E. 19th St.
63.	Payne, Raymond Lewis	18	1212 Ave. H
64.	Pierce, Wilbur F.	22	1031 E. 14th St.
65.	Pilkington, Addie	34	214 Webster Ave.
66.	Porter, Edward Erskine[e]	25	309 Caton Ave.
67.	Prout, Glover Perrin	38	35 Clarkson Ave.
68.	Rich, Alfred B.	63	153 Martense St.

69. Rothe, J. Ferdinand	40	311 E. 19th St.
70. Rubin, Max Harry	49	673 Flatbush Ave.
71. Russo, Mamie[g]	19	485 Gravesend Ave.
72. Ryan, Michael J.[d]	37	2163 Nostrand Ave.
73. Schaeffer, Harold Willard	17	2804 Farragut Rd.
74. Schwaan, Aline	24	95 Lenox Rd.
75. Scudder, Ethel	14	1212 Ave. Q
76. Shevit, Sadie	23	1741 E. 19th St.
77. Snyder, Josephine Hubert	19	499 E. 18th St.
78. Stephens, William Edwards	68	83 Rugby Rd.
79. Sturm, Adolf	42	118 E. 32nd St.
80. Sullivan, Margarette	19	2745 Bedford Ave.
81. Talvo, Genaro	38	2739 E. 14th St.
82. Ten Broecks, Floyd G.	46	1421 Glenwood Rd.
83. Thieben, John	37	426 Cortelyou Rd.
84. Thorn, Charles Clarence	57	2023 Caton Ave.
85. Townsend, Rachel[a, c]	67	Grand Ledge, Michigan
86. Vincenzo, Joseph[g]	27	493 Gravesend Ave.
87. Vincenzo, Louis[g]	25	493 Gravesend Ave.
88. Walker, Marion	17	1617 E. 10th St.
89. Walsh, Genevieve	18	4301 Church Ave.
90. Watts, Hazel	21	48 E. 32nd St.
91. Weed, Harry W.	46	1912 Ave. H
92. Weinberg, Morris[h]	48	1706 Bath Ave.
93. Woelfer, Charlotte	32	738 E. 21st St.

Note: The 93 individuals here identified have been confirmed through official records as fatal casualties of the Malbone Street Wreck. Various popular sources (e.g., almanacs, newspapers, etc.) cite different numbers as the final death count, numbers that range from 92 to as many as 103. It is entirely possible that more than 93 people died in the accident.

[a] Not from a Brooklyn address.

[b] Charles and Mabel Arena were the only married couple to perish in the Malbone Street Wreck. There were other fatally injured passengers who rode the train with their spouse but no other cases of both being killed.

[c] Margaret Cooper and Rachel Townsend were sisters who were visiting relatives in Brooklyn.

[d] Michael Gilbert and Michael Ryan were related to each other; they were also relatives of the author's mother.

[e] The deaths of Thomas Gilfeather and Edward Erksine Porter were cited in later manslaughter indictments returned against six BRT officials and employees.

[f] Garnet McMillan was a chief pharmacist's mate in the U.S. Navy assigned to the New York Naval Shipyard in Brooklyn.

[g] Joseph and Louis Vincenzo were brothers; Mamie Russo was their cousin.

[h] Morris Weinberg was a guard on the train, working the post between the second and third cars; he was the only BRT employee killed in the wreck.

TABLE C.2: FATALLY INJURED PASSENGERS BY AGE

Age	Men	Women	All
Under 16 years	0	2	2
17–19 years	4	8	12
20–20 years	11	12	23
30–39 years	12	10	22
40–49 years	16	5	21
50–59 years	6	2	8
60–69 years	2	2	4
70 and over	1	0	1
Totals	52	41	93

TABLE C.3: FATALLY INJURED PASSENGERS BY MARITAL STATUS

Status	Men	Women	All
Single	12	31	43
Married	40	7	47
Widowed	0	3	3
Totals	52	41	93

TABLE C.4: FATALLY INJURED PASSENGERS BY COUNTRY OF BIRTH

Country of Birth	Men	Women	All
United States	37	30	67
Germany	4	1	5
United Kingdom (except Ireland)	1	3	4
Ireland (36 counties)	2	2	4
' France	0	2	2
Italy	1	1	2
Russia	4	1	5
Spain	1	0	1
Sweden	1	0	1
Romania	1	1	2
Totals	52	41	93

Source: Data compiled from newspaper accounts, death certificates, and cemetery records.

APPENDIX D
Civil Settlements

TABLE D.1: Civil Settlements: A Partial Listing

Date	Party/action	Settlement
Fatal injuries		
Nov. 24, 1918	John M. Mills for the wrongful death of his sister, Emily Coady[a]	$500
Nov. 24, 1918	Louis Kirchoff for the wrongful death of his daughter, Clara Kirchoff[a]	$5,000
Feb. 21, 1919	Mrs. Laura V. Flahive for the wrongful death of her husband, James F. Flahive[a]	$20,000
May 20, 1919	Mrs. Eloise Knox Porter for the wrongful death of her husband, Edward Erskine Porter[b]	Unknown
May 21, 1919	Mrs. Anna D. Ten Broecks for the wrongful death of her husband, Floyd G. Ten Broecks[a]	$55,000
Aug. 13, 1919	Estate of Bessie Love; wrongful death[c]	$7,500
Oct. 8, 1919	Ethel K. Pierce for the wrongful death of her husband, Wilbur F. Pierce[c]	$30,000
Nov. 11, 1919	Melleville P. Harris for the wrongful death of his wife, Gertrude Harris[c]	$736
Dec. 1, 1919	Florence M. Thorn for the wrongful death of her husband, Charles C. Thorn[c]	$20,659
Dec. 17, 1919	Mrs. Mary F. Maloney for the wrongful death of her daughter, Lillian Maloney[a]	$12,000
Dec. 22, 1919	Lucy A. Enggren for the wrongful death of her husband, John W. Enggren[c]	$34,000
Dec. 22, 1919	Ethel C. Holmes for the wrongful death of her husband, George W. Holmes[a]	$40,000
Dec. 30, 1919	Estate of Glover Prout; wrongful death[a]	$16,500
Jan. 7, 1920	Neil Clifford for the wrongful death of his daughter, Louise M. Clifford[a]	$10,000

Nonfatal injuries

July 10, 1919	Walter Mander for injuries sustained[c]	$500
July 10, 1919	Aubrey Lovell for injuries sustained[c]	$175
July 10, 1919	Genevieve Byrne for injuries sustained[c]	$450
July 14, 1919	Humbert Vanozzi for injuries sustained[c]	$125
July 14, 1919	Joseph Doyle for injuries sustained[c]	$200
July 23, 1919	William Wisser for injuries sustained[c]	$750
Aug. 13, 1919	Helen Heiss for injuries sustained[c]	$250
Aug. 13, 1919	Frank Leibert for injuries sustained[c]	$500
Aug. 25, 1919	Helen M. Harley (wife of Charles E. Harley) for injuries sustained[c]	$7,500
Aug. 25, 1919	Charles E. Harley (husband of Helen M. Harley) for injuries sustained[c]	$1,000
Oct. 8, 1919	William Mellor for injuries sustained[c]	$10,000
Oct. 9, 1919	Nora L. Hayes for injuries sustained[c]	$2,000
Oct. 9, 1919	Pauline Biggio for injuries sustained[c]	$75
Oct. 15, 1919	Rosario Antoniello for injuries sustained[c]	$2,500
Oct. 18, 1919	James F. Lowery for injuries sustained[c]	$350
Oct. 27, 1919	Kathryn Cusack for injuries sustained[c]	$150
Dec. 30, 1919	Katherine Murphy for injuries sustained[c]	$500
Dec. 30, 1919	Lillian Anderson for injuries sustained[c]	$400
Jan. 7, 1920	Edward N. Fitzpatrick for injuries sustained[c]	$35,000
Apr. 19, 1920	Sylvia Ghelardi for injuries sustained[c]	$8,500
Dec. 7, 1920	Marie Castellani for injuries sustained[a]	$39,500
Dec. 24, 1921	Elizabeth Van Arsdale for injuries sustained[d]	$5,500

[a] Level of liability established in court by civil suit.
[b] Case settled out of court; amount of liability not known.
[c] Level of liability recommended by special master.
[d] Case settled out of court; amount of liability reported to court.

TABLE D.2: AVERAGE SETTLEMENT

Type of Injury	Men	Women	All
Fatal	$34,332	$7,462	$21,793
Nonfatal	4,860	5,611	5,269

Source: Data compiled from newspaper accounts and federal court records (U.S. District Court, dockets 15 and 19, National Archives, New York).

INDEX

Fifth Avenue Line, 44, 46, 51, 55–6, 79
Flatbush, xii, 6, 8, 11, 16, 20, 22
Flatbush Avenue, 8, 9, 11–15, 24–6, 55, 71, 74, 97
Flatbush Avenue Extension, 24
Flatbush Avenue Railway, 9
Flatbush Court: Flatbush Magistrate's Court, 74, 83–4
Flatiron Building, 102
Flower, Roswell P., 19
Forest Hills, 102
Forney, Matthias Nace, 18
Foster Avenue, 23
Fourth Avenue, 73
Franklin Avenue, 12, 14, 59–62, 78–9, 97
Franklin Avenue Shuttle, 97–100
Fulton Ferry, xii, 17
Fulton Street, 8, 17, 22, 25, 55
Fulton Street Elevated, 17, 19, 25, 45, 51, 58–61, 63, 78, 79, 97

Garrison, Lindley M., 91, 92, 100
Gilbert, Michael, 78
Gilbert (car manufacturing company), 54
Gilfeather, Thomas, 87
Gorman, Peter, 59, 60–1
Gove, William G., 79
Governors Island, 4
Grade Crossing Commission, 21–2
grade crossings: grade crossing elimination, 21–2
Grand Army Plaza, 25
Grand Avenue, 59
Gravesend Avenue, 50
Greater New York, 8
Greenwood Cemetery, xii, 51, 55
Griffing, L. G., 37

Hallock, John H., 86
Hammerstein. See Rogers and Hammerstein

Harold, Donald W., xiii, 95
Hayes, Rutherford B., 6
Holy Cross Cemetery, 40, 101
horse racing, 50
Hubbell, Charles Bulkley, 37
Huntington, N.Y., 101
Hylan, John Francis: views on public ownership of mass transit, 34, 83–4, 97; early career, 83–4; actions as committing magistrate, 83–6; Hylan Papers, 90; life after 1918, 102

Independent Subway System (IND), 100, 102
influenza epidemic. See Spanish influenza
Interborough Rapid Transit Company, 23, 25, 34, 56, 80, 83, 102
Inter-Continental Construction Corporation, 25

Jay Street, 71
Jenks, Justice Almet F., 86

Kings County, 6, 7, 11, 12, 16, 18, 21; population, 16; morgue, 77–8; district attorney, 79; courthouse, 84; grand jury, 85–6
Kings County Elevated Company, 16–20, 54
Kings County Hospital, 77–8
Kings Highway, 22, 46, 51, 53, 55, 56

Lancaster Rifles, 32
Lafayette Avenue (Brooklyn), 3
Lafayette Street (Manhattan), 37, 38
Lazansky, Justice Edward, 87, 90
Lewis, Anthony, 101

Oriental Hotel, 14
Oriental Point, 14
Orr, W. J., 33, 35, 37

Park Place, 62–3
Park Row, 20, 51, 56–7
Penn Fulton Hall, 33
Penn Station: Pennsylvania Station, 18
Pennsylvania Annex (ferry line), 17–18
Pennsylvania Railroad, 14, 18
Porter, Edward Erskine, 87
Post Office Building, 34
Prospect Hall, 33
Prospect Park, 6, 7, 11, 22, 24–5, 38, 48, 58, 71, 74, 98
Prospect Park and Coney Island Railroad, 8, 15, 20, 42, 50, 51
Prospect Park Southwest, 73
Prospect Park Station, 20, 25, 26, 64, 68, 71, 73, 98
PSC. See New York State Public Service Commission for the First District
Public Service Commission. See New York State Public Service Commission for the First District
Pullman, 54

Queens (borough), 24

R. E. Seamans Company, 102
Rogers and Hammerstein, 12
roof shield, 24
Roosevelt, Franklin D.: Roosevelt Administration, 3, 102
Rose Polytechnic Institute, 101
Ryan, Michael, 78

Saint Francis of Assisi (parish church), 76

Saint Joseph's College for Women, 76
Sands Street, 17
Sands Street Station, 17, 58
Santa Fe, N.M., 102
Schermerhorn Street, 84
Sea Beach Line, 9
Seidl's Famous Orchestra, 17
Sheepshead Bay, 21
Smith, Alfred E., 2, 77, 92
Smith, James N., 7
Smith, Lewis J., 87, 89
Snyder Avenue, 74, 76, 77, 83–4
Spanish influenza, 1, 2, 41, 77
Staten Island, 23
steam: steam engines, 18, 19, 22
Stephenson, 54
Stillwell Avenue, 41
Surf Avenue, 41
Sweet, Abram M., 7

tables, ix
Taft, William Howard, 34
Tammany Hall, 83
Tilden, Samuel B., 6
Tillary Street, 58
Titanic, RMS, xi
Thorn, Charles, 18
Tort Creditors' Legislative Protective Association, 92
Transit Authority. See New York City Transit
Turner, Michael, 53, 56, 57, 63, 65
turntables, 12

Union Elevated Railroad, 17, 54
Union Ferry Company, 17
Upper New York Bay, 9
U.S. Government: National Archives, xiii; National War Labor Board, 33–6, 38; Navy, 76; federal judge, 91; Secretary of War, 91;